Word

Only On Paper

This book is recommended reading for professionals working in the grief and bereavement field; college level psychology students; and support group members. Professors and educators; recommend this book to your students and receive a bulk discount along with a free copy for yourself, by contacting HarrietBocca@earthlink.net.

Advance Reviews

"Harriett Bocca's first (of many I'm sure) book, "Words Spoken Only On Paper," is gripping and poignant. A peek into the lives of two women as their relationship begins with devastating loss and melds into the closest of bonds found. Theirs is a relationship drenched in the deepest human sorrow. At times sharing dreamy ethereal thoughts of grief and terror, the reader learns better than to question the strength and love these two women share. Their story is one of raw coping and uplifting acceptance. Once you begin to read this book you will not be able to put it down!"

Lori C. – Special Educator

"This touching story of two women united by a shared loss embodies the old adage, 'A burden shared is a burden halved.' The friendship that grows as they grieve, gain strength from each other and learn to go on with their lives is truly inspiring."

Denise M. - Author

"I was fortunate to meet Harriet Bocca for the first time recently and listened to a few excerpts of this lovely book read by her in person. At first, I thought the subject matter would be too sad, Harriet had lost a son and Holly had lost a dear, good friend. After reviewing the book, I soon realized that it was not only a story about grief, but a heartwarming story of unconditional love and friendship between two extraordinary women a generation apart. I started reading the book one afternoon and after a few pages, could not put it down.

"Children are not supposed to die before their parents, but you will not find standard clichés of "Why me?" or "It was God's will" in this book. Closure was not an option as you can never close the door when a loved one dies.

"Together, Harriet and Holly were able to reflect, cherish and validate their memories of Bert through exchanged letters of shared joys and life's trial and tribulations for over 20 years. As they grieved together, each found healing in their journey. Their Words Spoken Only On Paper were honest and from their hearts, many times too painful to say out loud. Along with love and encouragement, there is humor woven through the pages of this book. Their descriptive writings take you to where they live and into their hearts as well.

"Both Harriet and Holly have found purpose in their life. Harriet, along with her husband, followed her dream of building a home at rural Summer Lake. Holly has found peace and happiness living her dream as wife and mother in beautiful Idaho.

"I enjoyed reading that Harriet has not finished yet; she has a lot more things she wants to do in her life."

Maggie K. – Educator

Words Spoken *Only* On Paper

An inspirational story of the evolution of grief and love shared by two women

Based on a true story

Harriet Bocca

Copyright © 2011, Harriet Bocca

All rights reserved. No part of this book may be reproduced, stored, or transmitted by any means – whether auditory, graphic, mechanical, or electronic – without written permission of both publisher and author, except in the case of brief excerpts used in critical articles and reviews. Unauthorized reproduction of any part of this work is illegal and is punishable by law.

ISBN 978-1-105-05070-1

First Edition

Harriet Bocca

Email – HarrietBocca@earthlink.net

About the Author

Harriet Bocca and her husband Don have been married for almost fifty years. They have worked together on their relationship, in business and in life.

She grew up in a small house with six siblings in San Fernando Valley, California. There she learned to adjust easily to sharing and the value of strong family ties.

With four children to raise and a busy household, Harriet involved herself in the activities of being a mom. Then in 1980, her oldest son died at age seventeen of a drug overdose. Harriet along with her whole family struggled to survive such a loss. Eleven years later, when the sting of such a tragedy was giving way to a brighter future, Harriet's nineteen year old son and youngest, died in a devastating accident. Paralyzed with grief she turned to writing. This is where she found a place to express her sorrow and longing and this is where she has dedicated her life in an effort to help others.

Through the years, she has been a member of many organizations and support groups. Her involvement with Soroptimist International and becoming a Hospice volunteer, where she worked with patients as well as children's bereavement art group were rewarding. However, her most recent passion is working with children in the foster care system. In 2005, she became a Court Appointed Special Advocate (CASA), which is a volunteer organization that helps give foster children a voice in court. As a CASA, Harriet has found purpose.

Harriet has written and published numerous articles about her experiences. She has also been asked to speak of her experiences. Her true passion is to try to help those who are in the grips of sorrow.

A Message From Harriet

Life is made up of bits and pieces of accumulated memories. We live and gradually learn from those bits and pieces, in an effort to find out who we are, what we came here for, and how we can make a difference.

This is a story based on bits and pieces of my life which I've wanted to tell for a long time. Most of all, it's a story of a special kind of friendship, defined by shared grief and longing. You will come to know two different women, one who faced the tragic death of two teenage sons, and the other traumatized by the death of her best friend.

Together we reached out to one another and helped fill a need in both. At first, we barely knew each other; and communicated through letters. These were simple **Words Spoken Only On Paper**, filled with pain and sorrow, yet always attempting to support. As the years passed and our lives continued the letters evolved into intimate and revealing feelings spilling out on paper. In our private bond of trust, we were safe thus allowing our hearts to speak without judgment. Unafraid, yet vulnerable, we grew stronger in our unspoken words, always sensitive with deliberate intent not to hurt or upset. We instantly knew that to speak the words aloud was just too painful.

Names and places have been changed, as I wish to preserve others' privacy. Some of the letters have been edited and words changed or omitted in order to maintain the continuity of the story. While I put this book together, I could not have completed nor even started without the generosity of the young woman I call Holly. She desires to remain anonymous yet has encouraged and contributed completely to our combined work of love. Through writing this book, I have come to realize that I am not alone in this life's journey, and what a journey this has been.

Dedication

This book is dedicated to my two sons who did not disappear from this earth without leaving a huge impact on those who knew them. Their lives held enormous meaning and their goodness was contagious.

To Mary & Floyd
With this book I give you part of my heart.
You are two special people
Thank you - With love,
Harriet Becca
Bonnie Regn

Acknowledgements

This book was written with the love and support of many people.

Thank you to sweet Holly, who gave me her soul and helped heal mine.

My husband, who has always been there, held me up and never let go.

My children, grandchildren and family who continue to support.

Thank you to Joan who had the patience and tenacity to help edit, always encouraging me to continue.

Thank you to Vicki who gave her professional input and shared her knowledge freely.

Also I must include those in my life who truly are friends, who have always been there and kept an eye on me and my entire family. Your kindness has been overwhelming.

Words Spoken *Only* On Paper

Words Spoken *Only* On Paper

Life is not perfect, for if it were, what goals would we have to attain and what dreams would we have to follow?

I live in a most incredible place, a place that at times seems to be part of God's own backyard. The wide-open spaces and expanse of this high desert terrain are interrupted only by an occasional white fluffy cloud floating across the clear blue sky. As my eyes gaze across the small fertile valley below, which is kept green by winter snowmelt, my vision is filled with the sight of massive jagged rock mountains. These mountains form part of the Sierra Nevada range and erupt thousands of feet high from the valley floor below. Here at Summer Lake I have found peace.

At five-thousand-feet in elevation I witness on a daily basis the inhaling and exhaling of God's own breath as He gives birth to the weather. Since much of this land is made up of volcanic rock, which retains the heat of the sun, His summer breath comes as a warm breeze, which caresses my body on a lazy afternoon. In the long winter months when the snowpack is heavy in the higher elevations, His breath turns icy cold and creates powerful turbulence in the heavens above. These strong storms make a winter wonderland for all who wish to enjoy. This isolated piece of earth I now call home, is where I've come to feel comfortable with my God and where I talk with Him. My personal intimate conversations are one sided and wrought with anger, often accusing Him of abandoning me. I sometimes scream at the top of my lungs, while standing out in the middle of His great outdoors…, so sure He would hear my voice and so focused on my needs that I could not

Harriet Bocca

Massive Jagged Rock Mountains

hear His. Only when I am peaceful and quiet do I hear a gentle voice. It's a voice of protection and in those special moments of silence, I feel most exposed yet cradled in His arms.

I did not come to this place by accident. The lifestyle I'm living evolved out of necessity and the tenacity to survive. In 1980 our seventeen-year-old son Brandon, died of a drug overdose. Shocked and overwhelmed with grief, including guilt, my husband Don and I knew we needed to find a place to feel safe. The toll, which the death of a child takes in a marriage and its relationship, is filled with sharp edges and silent moments of anguish. The temptation to disappear from life and the desperation to make everything all right for our family literally tore us apart. The need to provide a secure home for our remaining three children helped us hold onto life, or maybe life simply held onto us!

It was then that we found these forty acres of high desert covered with sage, sand, and rocks. This is where my husband and I came to let go of our feelings. Here we could work out our anger, fears, and deep grief. It became our safe place, a place away from pitying eyes of family and friends. We longed for the life we knew we would never have, the one where we all lived "happily ever after." We knew we would always be without. Our natural instinct to keep mentally and physically active served us well, as we never allowed the pain to catch up with us and become all-consuming.

Through the years we slowly began to accept that which we could not change, perhaps, I should say adjust. Our trips to this special place, which we now call home, gave us purpose and soon we found the energy to begin again. We started with tiny steps to develop the land by first clearing a spot to park our travel trailer. Each sage bush had to be dug up by hand, sometimes we had to twist around, and around almost like a corkscrew to succeed in removing them. After that, we struggled with huge boulders and rocks and an occasional snake, bunny rabbit, deer or witnessed majestic bald eagle flying over our heads. Then we tackled the project of sinking a well. It took many months of coordinating with a local well driller and with no guarantees of finding water; we finally hit water after four hundred feet of drilling. In celebration, we erected a windmill and planted trees. The work kept our minds busy and our bodies exhausted. Eventually we began to trust that we could dream again, that some things were in our control. We truly began to bond with the land, understanding that we were just temporary stewards in this temporary life.

Our dream was to build a little house and live in the wide-open spaces surrounded by nature and in the shadow of God's great arms. During these years, we had times when the wind in our lives would blow far too hard…these were the times when we held onto the sage, rocks, and each other…, so we would not blow away. Slowly as the years passed, our life began to flow into a rhythm of acceptance.

Words Spoken Only On Paper

Our remaining three children, who were deeply scarred by the death of their brother, began to build their own dreams and move on with their lives. Our son Laurence joined the Army and traveled the world, thanks to Uncle Sam. Anne, our only daughter, who was in her second year of high school, immersed herself in cheerleading and other school activities and our youngest son Bert became active in motorcycle racing with his dad. Don and I struggled through intimacy in our relationship and eventually began to allow our spirits to mend and our love to evolve. Change was in the wind, as we faced the rest of our lives following a new and different path. Those who have lost a child, at any age, will tell you that the sting of longing never goes away, but most realize that life must go on. We chose to continue, we had other children to think of…to live for and we had each other.

Eleven years later on a beautiful summer day, we found ourselves traveling on a business trip down the coast of California to a popular beach resort. Our excitement at having family and friends visit us, while we were in the area, was paramount in our minds. Our daughter, who was now married and had two children, had planned to join us for a few days. I would have fun seeing the grandchildren; she would enjoy a little vacation at the beach. Our youngest son Bert, who lived about three hours away, had mentioned that he might visit as well.

We arrived at the hotel and settled in for the night. The room was spacious and the feel of fresh sheets welcomed us as we crawled into bed. The loud ringing of the phone woke me out of my twilight comfort and our daughter's voice, trembling as she teetered on the verge of panic, telling me that there had been a motorcycle accident.

Harriet Bocca

Our son Bert, who was nineteen, had been involved. Someone from the hospital emergency room had called her in an attempt to reach us. She simply told us we needed to get to the hospital. We arrived at the emergency room in the middle of the night, the parking lot almost empty as we pulled in. Our headlights flashed on a person standing at the entrance. It was our daughter. As we got out of the car she came toward us, I knew by the look on her face and the way she walked that he was dead. I dropped to my knees, unable to stand and unable to breathe. We learned that Bert, our youngest son had died instantly of massive trauma to his head. The funeral was held the next week and again we faced the horror of the death of a child.

The Letters Begin

She was standing right behind me as the mourners passed by on that horrific day. Her arms filled with a beautiful bouquet of white roses and a card. His casket was off to my right, closed from view. The sweet smell of flowers filled the overflowing chapel and his favorite music could be heard from the sound system.

Numb, yet my mind filled with silent screams… "How can I get through this, how can I live a moment longer?" How can my family go through burying another brother, uncle, grandson, cousin, and another child of ours?" We were not new to this kind of grief; we had lived this nightmare before and the pain was part of us. The sadness was all-consuming.

My husband in silent sorrow squeezed my hand and never let go. The girl standing behind me never let go either. As she handed me a beautiful bouquet of white roses, her eyes were filled with tears and her nose was all red from crying. It's funny how you can remember the exact details of moments in your life, perhaps it's a survival instinct, something that your mind locks onto to divert you from absorbing reality. A small card with a hand written note was in her fragile shaking hand. It was the first, and one of many she would give me through the years. The note inside read;

Mrs. Bocca,

    Bert bought me white roses for my birthday last year, and he's not going to be here this year to give me any. He told me that you should always give white roses to the ones you truly care about, because everybody gets red ones, but white ones are special So, I wanted to share one of the special thoughts he had with you. He was a really neat person and had a good heart. I have never admired anyone so much as I do him. Out of all the phone calls we had, a few of them he told me how much he loved you and his dad and how he wanted to make you proud. I wanted you to know how

Harriet Bocca

much he loved you, because sometimes people forget to say it!

Sincerely, Holly

How could I have known when I read that first note that this would be the start of a relationship, which would sustain us both through the years? This young fragile seventeen-year-old girl would be my rock. Her words of kindness and unconditional love for my son would hold me up when I was close to falling. Our friendship evolved into a special bond, she maturing into a grown married woman with children, and I growing older, yet still fighting for purpose. Her letters, calls and occasional visits, eventually evolved into a loving friendship of two women facing life head on through the common denominator of a tragic loss. I buried my son that day and she buried not only her best friend, she buried part of her heart.

While she and my son had been friends for quite a while, they only dated for a few short months, after that their friendship seemed to evolve into a deeper level, one of trust and mentoring. I had met Holly once, yet Bert talk about her often and I knew she was very special to him. While he had many close friends who were more like family, she was different. Bert's friends, who were on the threshold of adulthood, took care of each other; they hung together, watched out for each other, and loved each other. They were no different from most young adults, trying so hard to grow up and not miss a moment. They had dreams of the future, dreams of always being together. However, when Bert spoke of Holly, it was not the same; their relationship was unique. Their shared respect for each other went beyond friendship. Later when they broke up, and she reunited with her former boyfriend, they stayed connected. Since she had moved a distance away, they often wrote letters and called each other. It was as if they were teaching and learning together, helping each other through life, stumbling along the way.

Bert's group of friends was traumatized by his death, holding vigils together while holding each other up. Day and night, they stood ready, giving, grieving, and praying that it was all unreal, that their friend had not died. Holly was there as well, more reserved, like a little flower fading into the forest.

She has remained there in my life, and has blossomed from a bud into the wonderful person she is today. Throughout the years, we have exchanged intimate and private thoughts through our letters. At first we struggled to find common interests, then as our relationship evolved, it grew into a trusting bond, much like my son's relationship with her must have been. In our letters, we exposed our vulnerabilities and became more like mother, daughter, mentor, and sisters. Our feelings and thoughts were not judged, as we learned to listen to each other's heart.

Harriet Bocca

The Death of Two

1980

Two! It might be a good number if you're talking two ice cream cones, one for each hand, or two new pairs of shoes, but not so good when you're talking about the fact that two of your children have died. Both were teenagers and doing things which every parent, at one time or other, fears. I know they were risk takers, as they took big bites out of their short lives. They loved riding motorcycling, competing in sports, or just about anything outdoors. Oftentimes I would hear about their antics, and as any mother would, I voiced my concern, nagging about the fact that they had only one body and one life, so "don't damage it beyond repair."

As most teenagers do, they struggled with making good and bad choices; after all, they were invincible! Regretfully their bad choices cost them their lives. When I think back and rehash everything that happened and how they lived their lives, I realize that they had a great life. Perhaps that's why they died so young, as it might not have gotten any better. Both had good friends, were outgoing, and well loved. We as parents, tried to teach by example and our long-term marriage must have given both a strong sense of stability that not all children have.

So why . . . ? This is a question we've asked ourselves many times, but perhaps the question should not be why, but why not? After all, life is fragile, dangerous, and definitely temporary!

Words Spoken Only On Paper

Brandon at age seventeen chose to experiment with drugs. As parents we knew so little about street drugs. We were so ignorant, stupid and in such denial. In retrospect we should have known, should have realized, should have, would have, could have……..

Early one Saturday morning, when the house was very quiet I was awakened by screams coming from upstairs. The inaudible words of terror were from our daughter and son Laurence. All I could understand was…"he's not breathing…he's not breathing!"

My husband Don had gotten out of bed early to do a "honey do" job in the garage and heard the screams as well. We both ran up the stairs and into our son's room. There he lay on his bed, dressed in shorts and shirt. He was very still and his face was the color of ash. Our instincts kicked in as we frantically instructed our children to call 9-1-1. Together we attempted to resuscitate him. As Don started chest compressions, I put my mouth to his, feeling the softness of his lips as I tried desperately to kiss him back to life. This was my first child, the one who cried the day he went to kindergarten, admitting he missed home. The one who had convinced his younger brother, Laurence that they could be like the dare devil Evel Knievel and ride their bikes off jumps high into the air. This was our son, who had an enormous amount of compassion and who gave away his smile to strangers. With his red hair and freckles you couldn't help but notice him when he walked in the room. He just seemed to make the room brighter.

Later we found out that Brandon had taken off work early the night before and had gone to a party. His friends saw that he got home;

we didn't even hear them help him up the stairs. In my heart I know they wanted to keep him out of trouble and for sure didn't want us to find out he had been doing drugs! I know they thought the drugs he took the night before would just wear off. Their protection was misguided; a decision they have had to deal and come to grips with for the rest of their lives. The reality is that they were just kids and trying to help a friend.

Our community and family held us up as we buried him, many feeling like their own child had died, many realizing that it could have been their own child! The day after Brandon died; I found Don curled up in a fetal position on our bed dealing with his grief in his own way. Cards and letters poured in and slowly the shock and pain dulled. Every morning I would get up and sit in the living room with a cup of coffee. There on the fireplace mantel was Brandon's high school graduation picture, (he died just before graduation), and there I would visit with him. I loved these intimate quiet moments with him; I felt I was not through as a mother, I knew I would never be through and that I would always be his mom. I would work until exhaustion, sometimes finding myself driving around in the neighborhood and feeling lost. In my wandering, I would search for a pull-out off the road that was away from prying eyes. I needed a quiet place to grieve, to talk with my son as only a mother can.

Day after day we would continue our routine, sometimes in a fog, sometimes not talking, but going through the motions of living, pushing through the numbness. The nights were unbearable, as sleep would not spare us from our reality. The clock ticked, one second at a time…sometimes it was very slow and very loud!

Eleven Years Later

1991

 They say that time heals all. Who are they? Okay, things did get better. They had to! We had three other children who needed to have a life, a life with a father and mother who could actually function. Laughter slowly crept into our life again, sometimes quite unpredictable, allowing us to be distracted as we struggled to cope. I knew the most important thing I could do was to keep it together. There was no time or energy for a pity party; people get tired of the pity party crap anyway. They want you to move on, so they can move on. It takes a lot of energy to be sad all the time and enormous stamina to be around a sad and depressed person, especially a grieving mother or father. What can any person do or say? Those closest to us kept in touch, some faded away, perhaps uncomfortable with themselves or us. I kept busy. Busy is good as it helps pass the time and keeps your mind occupied. We all tried to move on. Oh, how I hate those words!

 The other word I hate is closure, which means end, shut down or finish. Excuse me, how can any parent, shut down, or ever finish the life of their child? Memories of the hopes, dreams, and potential of their child can live on forever. I'd much rather think of getting through and thriving, making a difference because of the loss, learning the lesson and validating that their life held enormous meaning.

Harriet Bocca

Well, we did get through the death of Brandon and we did "move on"…but there is never closure, as this grief work has no door.

Then the phone rang as we slept in our hotel room that night. It was such a peaceful place with the cool ocean breeze making sleep welcoming. As I processed the words our daughter Anne was saying, "Bert had been in a terrible motorcycle accident and we needed to get to the hospital right away" I felt my heart skip a beat and then silent panic.

We made the trip to the hospital in a record-breaking three hours, speeding down the Los Angeles Freeway. There was not much traffic at that late hour, guess most people are either still at the bars or nightclubs, or home in bed. All I remember is how the black asphalt with broken white lines rushed by and seemed to be hypnotizing. I tried to focus on that road, not what might lie ahead. My thoughts were on plans for recovery. I could take care of our son for as long as it took, Don would have to travel and work alone. Our family would all help, our son would be OK, he would be able to go on with his life, and we would get through this! Our daughter and her husband met us in the parking lot of the hospital. The moment I saw her face, I knew. It was as if time stood still, and the picture in my mind cemented forever, I got out of the car and took one-step at a time to reach her. My legs were like cement, my mind frozen in fear yet the need to reach our daughter; to find out … kept me moving. Don held me in his arms, he as shattered as I, yet forever strong. There we stood, arms around each other, struggling to hold each other up. I would not have liked to witness this scene, as it's the one you see on TV far too often, that of a family devastated and broken.

As we entered the double doors of the emergency room, I could see people sitting around in chairs. When our eyes met there was a look of forbearing exchanged. It was as if they knew, they could tell. We were the family that needed to be taken care of. After all, it must not have been hard to recognize our pain. A nurse, who was standing by the workstation, escorted us to a small room. There a doctor had been ready to give us the vital information of our son's death. Looking back on those moments I have a new respect for emergency room staff, who not only have the enormous task of dealing with medical emergencies, but comforting families who may be traumatized by their catastrophic words. Each moment that ticked by is embedded in my mind, it's part of me. From the shape of the counter as we entered the emergency room, the glass windows which allowed a view of outside and the color of the chair in the small intimate room, where denied reality was recognized. I think this vivid memory of the mundane was my survival instinct, a way to divert my mind from the unacceptable. It was as if things happened in slow motion….then time stopped. At first, the small intimate room was quiet and still and I had the feeling we were isolated and away from others. We were told that the chaplain was on his way and someone asked if I wanted something to help… a pill of some kind. My mind raced, would a pill make this go away?

I stood up and slowly walked to the bathroom, which was nearby. There in that small dark room, and all by myself, I became more primate than human. The sound, which I made, came from something else, an unknown entity deep inside, and a place where human living beings are afraid to go, must not go. It was a non-recognizable animal sub human sounds …it was a guttural sound of dying.

After…..after I died in that little dark room, I knew I had to pull myself together, literally! That night is still suspended in my mind, much like a movie scene frame by frame in slow motion and without sound. I needed to reach our son Laurence, who was still at our house in the mountains. He needed us as bad as we needed him. It was a long silent drive up the mountain that night, Laurence was waiting at the front door, his face, and eyes red from crying. I kept singing in my head, "I love you, I love you, I love you." These were the only words I could allow in my head, something to put there, when nothing else was acceptable. Sleep was not possible, yet we tried. Don gathered a couple of our sleeping bags and spread them out on the living room floor. There we laid in silence, I kept looking at the fan above, as it went round and round, while repeating the same words, "I love you, I love you, I love you!" It was as if I had to say goodbye.

Morning came slowly and turned out to be bright and sunny. I kept wondering how it could be so nice, when it was so dark. I knew our family was on their way, rushing throughout the night, trying to reach us. I knew I needed everyone; I just needed them with me, with us. I knew they would be in shock and would have to struggle with our loss as well as theirs. When I looked out the window, I could see several cars parked in the driveway and up the street, recognizing our friends who must have heard of the accident in the middle of the night.

Small communities are like that, these friends held vigilance, wanting to help and not knowing how. Many were the same friends who eleven years earlier gathered around to hold us in their arms when Brandon died. It was more like déjà vu as they continued their vigil for days.

The circumstances, which led to Bert's death, were in his control. Like his brother Brandon, he was at a Friday night party, surrounded by friends, having fun. All were on the edge of life, teetering between the innocence of youth and wisdom of maturity. The waters are rough during this time of life, as many find themselves floundering in an attempt to keep from drowning. Alcohol was the beverage of choice, shoring up their insecurities. Bert made the choice to drink and then get on that motorcycle. We later learned his friends had tried to stop him, knowing he shouldn't drive. It wasn't the mountain that got in his way when he slammed into the side of it, he knew how to handle a motorcycle, it was his bad choices that got in his way, and took his life.

The experts refer to grief as "grief work," how right they are. How would we survive the death of another son and how could we possibly work that hard? We were worn out, and had been in this dark place before. I wanted to crawl in a hole and never come out, but somehow people kept pulling me.

Harriet Bocca

August 1991

Dear Holly,

What an absolute sweetheart you are. The white roses were so special. I didn't get a chance to talk with you much at the funeral. There were so many people, but I know you were one of the special friends of Bert's. He saved all the letters you wrote and I should return them, but I can't bear to part with them just yet. Please forgive me for reading them but I had to, they were beautiful and full of good friendship. Please take care of yourself, Bert would want that. You know, make smart choices; you're too special not to be happy.

Thank you for giving Don and me so much. I'll write later and send back your special letters.

Love, Harriet and Don "Bert's mom and dad."

September 1991

Dear Holly,

As you can see, I've written to you and had the wrong address. Enclosed you'll find some envelopes that Bert had addressed to you when he was here in Sacramento. As you know he loved to customize envelopes, some pretty far out there. I'm also finally sending some of the letters you had written to him. When I read them I felt part of his life.

You have so much love in your heart. I know someday you'll find that special someone who will care for you and love you the way you deserve. Don't settle for anything less. By the way, I still have the beautiful picture of you that he had on the dashboard of his truck. May I keep it?

Think of Bert as a part of your growing up life and someone who will always be handy to talk to, now even more than ever. I'm sure he has a long list of people wanting to get in touch with him, but I know you will be at the top of his list. Try not to cry too much Holly; it takes from your beautiful smile.

Love, Harriet and Don

October 1991

The package arrived less than two months after Bert died. I was quite surprised to find something fun to open instead of the usual bills. When they say, "life goes on," I guess that's the kind of life they mean. The return address on the package was from our son's friend Holly.

Enclosed in the package was a simple sweet card. On the front it said, "You're on my mind..., and in my heart." Inside the handwriting was neat and clear, thanking me for returning the special letters she had mailed to our son before he died. I had found them in his drawer and since they were so personal I knew she would like them back. Her note read:

Harriet Bocca

On Bert's birthday, my mom and I went to the cemetery and put flowers there. It had been exactly two months since the accident, but it seems so much longer than that to me. I think because I have really missed his friendship. I have enclosed some letters that he had written to me. I don't know if you want to read them, but I wanted you to have the choice. They really are Bert. They show exactly who he was and some of his thoughts that he rarely shared. They show what a wonderful friend he was to everyone, and mostly they show what a beautiful heart he had. There are some bad words in between all the goodness, but that's Bert too.

Even though it is still hard to accept and I miss him very much, I have a lot of faith that he is happy and that's good to know. It is the ones left behind that are sad, but I find comfort in knowing that wherever he is, there is probably a grin on his face.

Thanks again for writing to me. Your letters made me smile all day long,

Love from Holly

Words Spoken Only On Paper

November 1991

Dear Holly,

How lucky Bert was to have such a good friend in you. Do you know that you were the only girl he ever wanted me to meet? He always had lots of girls calling him, but you were different. He worried about you. You know he's still looking out for you right now. He wants you to be happy and safe, get an education and be independent. I'm sure he would want you to eventually get married and have a family. Yep, life must go on and we will all be happy someday and keep him in our hearts.

Don and I read the letters you sent that Bert wrote. It was fun to be part of his life (as only his friends could be), for a moment or two. It's too bad we had to be his parents, as it would have been so much fun to be a friend he hung out with. We might have even developed a taste for his music and not just thought it was loud and annoying. Having said that, we know that as parents we played a different role, we were the ones who he needed for guidance and example. Apparently, we could have done better.

Last week we sold his truck and I must admit it was quite emotional. The guy who bought it has plans to fix it all up and trick it out, that would have made Bert happy. Our daughter and her family will be moving to Sacramento in a few weeks, they wanted to be closer to us. It will be nice to have family around as it's been very quiet around here. Laurence, his wife and our new grandbaby will be here for

Harriet Bocca

the Thanksgiving Holiday. It will be good to see our dinner table filled with those we love. It's apparent that life does go on, no one has ever said it would be easy and as a matter of fact, it's been pretty "shitty"! Our past is past, but we have tomorrow.

Don and I have been fortunate we have survived…so far, not many would be able to cope with such a devastating loss twice. One thing that helps is to know that our boys had a great life as kids, perhaps it was their time to leave, just not our time to see them go.

I'll be sending back your letters in a few weeks. Thank you for being so thoughtful. Bert would be so happy knowing that we are all staying close. His whole group of friends has been so supportive, including their parents. The letters and calls have touched our heart. It's what helps keep us going forward, back can be too painful.

Please keep in touch, even if it's just once a year as your life will continue to evolve and change. Please do not lose us, dear Holly.

Love, Harriet and Don

December 1991

The first Christmas after a death is always difficult, so when we received this small package just days before Christmas, my heart felt lighter. It was wrapped carefully in fabric with the hand painted gift of an angel tucked inside. The Christmas card was the scene of cute animated cartoon characters setting in front of a fireplace hearth with stockings hanging from a nail. Mylar confetti hearts fell all over the kitchen table as I opened the thoughtful card.

Harriet and Don,

I hope this made it in time for the holidays; I was a little late in sending it. As you can see, I took up painting as a hobby. I am happy to announce that I am expecting a baby and while Tony and I haven't set a date for the wedding, we wanted you to know the good news, we're so excited and can't wait.

All my love, Holly

Dear Holly,

How exciting to bring a new life into this world, I can't be happier for you. I think back of the time when I found out I was expecting our first child, Brandon. Not married and unprepared, both Don and I struggled to figure out what to do. Of course, at that time in our history society looked down on unwed mothers. We struggled with our relationship and how to tell our families. Eventually we did the right thing for us and got married. Our parents were terrific; my dad sat me down on his lap and told me everything would be all right and they would help as much as they could. Don had just gotten a job, which took a lot of pressure off, financially. We still had a lot of growing up to do, who doesn't at eighteen? It's a lot better for a single parent now. I believe there must have been a lot of young girls back then who did things they later regretted, under the pressure of family and society.

Warm regards dear Holly; and congratulations. Please let us know everything about the upcoming event.

January 1992

Life does go on, and on with good things too! We received the news that Holly had a beautiful baby girl, and all was well with mommy and child. I wanted to send something thoughtful to this new mommy, who was such a special friend to my son. I found the perfect little rocking chair and some nursery rhymes on tape, which she could sing to her baby. I also sent an assortment of tea, hoping Holly would have quiet time to enjoy when the baby slept. Perhaps I should say, if the baby slept?

Words Spoken Only On Paper

March 1992

Dear Holly,

    What a nice surprise to find your cheerful letter upon my return from Southern California. I loved the artwork, you're quite talented. Thank you for making me smile.

    I ran into Jimmy back home in the mountains and he looked so good and seemed to have such a positive attitude. Seems he's been writing to you and your shared letters help him feel better. You, my dear, are giving him something to be happy about and listening to him. You did the same for Bert; good people make those around them feel good.

    Don and I have more or less been on the road since January. I love to travel with him, just not all the time. Good thing he loves his work or it would be a real job! Now that we're home here in Sacramento I've been busy with grandchildren. How I miss their hugs and kisses, they always make me feel needed. Speaking of kids, I bet Nicolet is starting to scoot around on the floor by now. Before you know it she'll be walking, which is why you have babies when you're young, imagine how they can wear you out when you're older.

    Don and I will be driving over the Sierras to Summer Lake next week. It's time to turn on the water system, fix fences, move rocks, (the ones the wind moved) and chase the deer away so they don't chew into our water lines! Perhaps one day you will be able to come and see what we've accomplished. Next Labor Day we expect about twenty of Bert's friends for our Annual Barbecue. I miss having teenagers around so it will be fun and emotional for me. It's almost like they are coming to protect us. Now… where are they going to sleep? I forgot to tell them we have rattlesnakes! Sleeping on the ground in tents would not be so good. Their plan is to all pitch in and drive a motor home and some will get rooms at the local lodge.

Take care and know you will always be close to my heart,

Love, Harriet

April 1992

Dearest Harriet,

Sorry that it has taken me so long to get back to you. As you know, babies keep you very busy! I wanted to thank you for the baby gifts. Our new daughters' name is Nicolet and of course she is beautiful, sweet and everything. She and I both love the nursery rhymes; they lull us both to sleep.

I have enclosed some pictures of Nicolet; hope you can see her in person one of these days. I am supposed to be in the Sacramento area sometime in late May. I would really love to get together while I am there.

I wanted to tell you that Bert's friend Jimmy has recently seen your new granddaughter and said she is cute. I bet she is getting big. I never realized just how fast babies grow and how much they change your life!

Well, please keep in touch; I look forward to your letters.

Love from Holly, Have a Great Easter

Dear Holly,

Thank you for sending the photos of Nicolet. She is so precious and has your beautiful eyes. Don and I feel privileged to be included in your life and now hers. Babies grow so fast, enjoy every moment, and take lots' of pictures. Keep healthy cuz she's gonna keep you running. Jimmy is a sweetheart and yes, he's right about our granddaughter, she is a cutie…guess that's grandma talking. Enjoy your first Easter with Nicolet, give her a couple of years and she'll find every egg the Easter Bunny hid.

Love, Harriet

Harriet Bocca

June 1992

Dearest Harriet,

    This new mommy stuff really keeps me busy. Our trip up to Sacramento had to be canceled because we had a death in the family. We'll try to make the trip another time I was looking forward to seeing you and Don and show off our little Nicolet.

    I had a very long, good conversation with Jimmy recently. He says he sees your son Laurence with his new daughter and can't get over how adorable she is. He also said that he missed you and Don. I hope that I am not overstepping my boundaries, but I really think that Jimmy would be very happy to hear from you. He said he sees you when you're in town, but it's not the same. Maybe a special note just to say Hi-how are you?!

    Well, all is good here, Nicolet is healthy, and we expect her to start crawling any day. Since we've moved to the desert I find it uncomfortably hot. I sure miss the cool mountain air.

Please continue to keep in touch and maybe we can get together around the 4th. Let me know.

Love from Holly

Harriet Bocca

Nicolet Crawling Along the Floor

Words Spoken Only On Paper

Dear Holly,

I'm sorry for your recent loss, we hope you have wonderful memories and can focus on them when things get tough.

I love to hear about your Nicolet. I remember how much fun it was when my baby's started crawling. I believe it makes you a better housekeeper as little ones scoot along the floor cleaning it with their knees. Of course, you have to wash all their outfits.

I agree with you about missing the cool mountain air. Sacramento is unbearably hot in the summer time, but we do get a cool delta breeze in the evening. I will get in touch with Jimmy; I know he looked up to Bert like a big brother. In fact, I had a talk with Jimmy's parents about how close the boys were…they said they loved Bert too. I know there are many people in our lives who have suffered from his tragic death, so many of his friends (you) have been deeply affected. I only hope that the lessons of life were learned and it has made a difference. I can't even talk about how our two remaining children will carry this pain forever. I only hope they remember the laughter in their lives.

Take care my dear; give Nicolet a big sloppy kiss.

Harriet Bocca

September 1992

Dear Harriet,

    Our beautiful daughter, Nicolet is almost walking now. I have to be on my toes as she gets into everything.

    I hope the weather in Sacramento isn't as hot as the desert down here. I've always heard that Sacramento cools down at night. Seems like this far south all it does it stay hot and windy. We got a chance to go camping last weekend at the Kern River near Bakersfield, California. It was so pretty with all the green trees, which I really miss. What a difference from the desert.

    My Birthday was on August 18, but I didn't really do anything special. While I am now nineteen, I feel a lot older than that. I really would have liked to go to your Annual Deep Pit Barbecue this weekend, as I have great memories of vacationing at Summer Lake with my family Bert and I always thought that it was so weird you buying property there, since hardly anybody has heard of it!.

Words Spoken Only On Paper

Well, please write back if you get the time, I always look forward to your letters,

Love, from Holly

My dear Holly,

    Don and I camped on the Kern River years ago; I think Bert was about one and Brandon almost ten. Laurence and Anne, being born so close together, were just seven and eight. They had a ball playing in the sand and watching baby trout swimming in the pools. The river was wild and very swift at our location so it was a tedious job keeping an eye on them, we heard too many stories of people being swooped up by the current and having to be rescued down river. Anne had severe asthma when she was young, so she wasn't as adventuresome as the older boys. She and Bert were happy to be playing in the sand and getting their feet wet in the shallow pools. I agree with you about the beautiful green trees at the Kern River. It did remind me of the years we lived in the mountains. When you were there, did you roast marshmallows? That was one of our favorite things to do while sitting around the campfire. Looking back at the good times we had, validates to me, that we had fun as a family and built many good memories. Of course camping is usually more work, but so different from being at home washing dishes in the dishwasher. I was always on alert for dangers when we were in the great outdoors, kids seem to do the craziest things. I have to ask myself why I didn't watch them more closely when they were teenagers. I also know that I was not able to be in control of all their actions once they reached that age. I thought our example as parents who tried to guide them would be enough when they had to make decisions.

We would love to see you make it to our Annual Deep Pit Barbecue, as each year we have more and more fun. Good thing we have lots of room for motor homes and campers, since many of our friends stay three or four days! Our Saturday night potluck dinner is outstanding with everyone pitching in and helping. You'll have to experience it.

Take care and enjoy every minute as a mommy, Hugs and love,

Harriet

October 1992

What a beautiful time of the year. Sacramento is full of color. The leaves are bright yellow, orange, and even some red. We had our first rain yesterday, which brought snow to the local mountains. That's not surprising for the Sierras and soon the ski resorts will be gearing up for the long winter and thousands of skiers.

Last weekend we drove to our little place at Summer Lake. I don't know if I ever told you but we planted a little experimental vineyard a number of years ago and it's time to put the vineyard to bed for the winter. I love to work and tidy up after the long summer. We originally planted sixty vines, each one a labor of love. The time spent nurturing them has always been good therapy for us, peaceful and serene with just the elements as distractions. If it's too hot, cold or windy, you can find me in our little travel trailer reading a good book or writing a letter.

Speaking of windy, we were lucky this year at our Annual Deep Pit Barbecue because the weather was perfect. It's always difficult trying to entertain over seventy five people in the wind. Someday our dream to have a little house where we can be protected and entertain our friends and family in comfort will happen, we just have to keep our dream alive.

Don and I recently went to a get together of some of Bert's friends down in Southern California. It was good to see them; they remain close to each other and help support each other. Some are still struggling with the reality of his death and acting out in ways that aren't in their best interest. I worry about them and have met with their parents to see if we can help in any way. Bert would not have wanted his death to destroy them, if anything he would want them to learn from his mistake. I must admit the sting of his death is still so sharp. I really can't believe more than a year has gone by. I miss him so much, there is a real physical pain. I've lost two beautiful, warm-hearted sons and I still survive. I guess by having all of you in my life helps me feel less isolated. Thank you.

With love, Harriet

Harriet Bocca

February 1993

Tampa Bay, Florida

Dear Holly, enclosed please find our New Year Letter. As you know, we send them out after the holidays, as it's so much better to answer all the Christmas letters at once. In reality, I don't particularly like the holidays, as you can well imagine. However, I love to get the notes and letters in the cards as they make me feel like I had a personal visit with each person. As the New Year Letter tells, our son Laurence and his wife will be having another baby sometime this month, or any minute! Here I sit in Tampa anticipating a call with the good news. Since this was a business trip, (not a bad business), I felt compelled to attend with Don.

It's absolutely stunning here. We're fortunate to be staying at an Inn which is on the bay, and I'm sitting poolside. I can see boats out in the channel and beautiful waterfront houses surround us. It's not a bad way to live, at least in the winter. I'm not sure if I would like the summers as I've heard that the humidity can be brutal. We've made many friends who work in Don's industry and many are down here for a seminar and trade show. It's a lot of fun getting together and hanging out with people from so many areas of this country.

March 1993

Dear Harriet,

Nicolet had her first birthday on January 10th so she's a big girl now or so she thinks!

Guess I don't have to ask if you have been busy, since you and Don are always traveling here and there for business. It just seems like you are always enjoying each other.

I'm not sure if you know how close Jimmy and I have become since Bert died. In fact, Bert was the one who introduced us and we have found support in each other. We each miss Bert in our own way and can share our memories.

Thank you for calling Jimmy after his recent accident, it meant a lot to him. He has a whole lot of sadness in his heart and

Harriet Bocca

Happy Birthday Nicolet

struggles with the reality that Bert has died. Their friendship was special; Jimmy looked up to Bert like a big brother. It helps when he talks to you. It helps me too, so thanks!

Easter is coming up; do you and your family have plans? We are having a barbecue at my mom's. There are always lots of babies running around in my family, so it should be fun for Nicolet. I hope your Easter is nice.

Love, from Holly

Dear Holly,

Isn't it amazing how important family becomes when you aren't together often? Before you had Nicolet, you might have wanted to go camping with friends or hang out with them instead of spending a day with family. Now that you're a mommy you can step back and see the value of all those who love you and how they support you. Of course knowing you, most of your friends are like family.

I do worry about Jimmy, he did think of Bert as a big brother. I'm so glad that you can open your heart to his pain, he needs a real friend right now.

Harriet Bocca

Don and I do travel a lot and yes, we have fun, but you have to know that we have moments of such sorrow; we withdraw from each other and avoid talking about our feelings. We struggle, yet we work hard to keep it together. Sometimes a thought of one of my boys will cross my mind and I will get hot and unable to breath. I once saw a boy about the age of seventeen crossing the street. He reminded me so much of Brandon, red hair and all, that I was compelled to stop. I wanted to see him up close; I wanted it to be him, I wanted him to be alive! I believe this would be construed as a woman who is crazy with grief. I was overwhelmed with emotions, but kept on driving, knowing that it was my need to see my son again, and not actually my son. I believe most people who have had a significant loss of a loved one have these moments. Grief can consume you but I've come to believe that perhaps at the very moment you are so overwhelmed with this longing to have them with you, at this moment they are closest to you.

Your letters always stir emotions in me; you have given me a voice on paper. I love you for your big open heart. I know that's what Bert loved you for, now go make dinner.

Love Harriet

April 1993

Dear Harriet,

   Thanks for your last letter; I am always really thrilled to get them. I wanted to write to say happy Mother's Day. I know you're not my mother, but you are really special to me, so I just wanted to let you know. Are you and Don still out and about traveling around? Have you had good weather, it doesn't seem to be able to decide between spring and summer here. Nicolet loves the sunshine because she likes being outdoors.

   I seem to be going through sort of a down phase lately. I've been thinking a lot about Bert, more than usual. I am always thinking about what life would be like if he was here. Guess I just miss him a lot. He was the best friend to have in the world, and I think I just need that right now. Does it get easier for you? Because I can't seem to get past it no matter how much time goes by, it really is a huge part of my life. Then I think of you and I feel so selfish. You seem so strong, I wish I had that

Harriet Bocca

strength. I am so thankful that I know you. You make me smile!

Love, from Holly

Oh, Holly, how my heart hurts for you.

As always Holly, you write so sensitive and pure. Mother's Day is, and has always been, difficult. I can't think of anything more painful than to participate in such a celebration when there is a big part of me, half of my children, are not with me. Yet I do have joy that they were mine, and always will be part of me. I still have two children who need me as a whole person in their lives. So here I am!

Yes, it feels like it just happened, but I have longer and longer periods of time that it's not so heavy on my heart. Of course, I go through down time when I think back about each last moment. Our last hug, our last kiss our last everything. I remember how warm Bert's back was when I last hugged him; he had driven out to the desert to join us for breakfast and had stood in the hot morning sun. His last breakfast with his family was blueberry pancakes.

You were so young to have experienced such a traumatic shock. Your friendship was special and I know Bert loved you, but most of all he respected you. Believe me I would be honored if I were your mother, at least a second mother. My mom died many years ago, and Don's mother is nice but emotionally distant. While Laurence and Anne send gifts and cards, it's a day I try to ignore. I believe once you're a mother, you're always a mother. So all the holidays, when families gather around, I feel emptiness. This doesn't mean I don't try but deep inside and in quiet moments I want to be with all my children.

I believe this is a human feeling, so don't be afraid to express yourself. It's alright to be sad and down in the dumps for a while. Don't let sadness linger in your life too long. It will wear you out and everyone who is around you, besides you've got a big, wonderful life ahead of you. Keep going forward, Holly and so will I.

I wanted to tell you one last thing. I've been reading a great book by Dr. Brian Weiss, about past life regressions. I really believe we have many lives and we learn different lessons as we go through those lives. Dr. Weiss talks about his experiences with some of his patients and this process. I believe we keep together with our loved ones through our many lives. I know this might sound a bit strange to some people; perhaps they are not comfortable with a different belief than what they were taught. It's hard to accept something which is so foreign to them and not popular.

So you see, I have great comfort in knowing that my boy's chose us to be their parents, perhaps their deaths were the lesson we had to learn. Now they have gone on to teach someone else or learn more, it's one big circle until we get it right.

Love, Harriet (your other mother)

Harriet Bocca

September 1993

Dearest Harriet,

It's been hot here in the desert, but has been beautiful at night. Since I've taken a part time job, I've been especially busy. Of course, Nicolet is all consuming, but I love it. She is the most beautiful part of life I have experienced.

I went to Bert's grave in August. I hadn't been there since his last birthday. I was nervous to go, I thought maybe it would be too hard, but I sat there and cried, but no more than usual. I did not feel very close to him there. I know his body is there, but I think I discovered that that is not where "Bert" is. He's in the mountains, he's riding his bike, he's definitely with his friends, and he's everywhere. I have been with him, he's in my heart. It isn't his body I miss; it's just him, his soul. Sometimes I forget his face and what he looks like and get really upset and frantically look for a picture. Then I get this overwhelming guilt inside. I love him so much, how could I forget what he looks like? But I think maybe it's okay, because I never forget him. You know what I never forget? I never forget that he is the only person who has ever loved me unconditionally. Even my parents have felt disappointment or shame about me, but never Bert. I only wish I could have told him, thank you. He had a genuine pure, good heart. I feel this same love from Nicolet. Sometimes I feel like Nicolet came into my life when Bert left it to give me something to love and take care of. Sometimes I think that his death would have destroyed me if I didn't have her. I can't go a day without thinking of him and sometimes I wish I could just forget about him or I am going to go crazy with grief, and what-ifs, and just thinking about and missing him...is this wrong?

I am a very strong believer in fate, everything happens for a reason. I still can't see the reason for his death yet, but if what you say is right, I am looking forward to our souls meeting again!

My birthday was really nice. My whole family was together for the occasion. It was my sisters 16th and my 20th, so it was a big party. My mother is finally in love and happy after all these years. This past Christmas is the first I have gotten to spend with my mom and dad together since I was two. It was so nice not having to choose where to go for which holiday. This is the first time I have ever felt like everybody I love is okay. I hope your family is the same.

Love always, Holly

October 1993

Dear Holly,

Your words were so tender and sweet it's no wonder Bert loved you. He knew you had a good soul and he needed you in his life. You were the first girl to take his heart. How lucky I am that you give me that gift back with each letter you write.

    I'm sorry that it's still so painful for you and I understand the panic feeling. Guilt and I walk a very dark long road sometimes. Deep in my heart I know I must not allow it to consume me, because I know it would destroy me as well as those I love. Do not let it destroy you!

Words Spoken Only On Paper

I know one thing, Nicolet is a lucky little girl to have you for a mom. I loved the picture of her in her little red and white jumpsuit. Her expression is so serious and so grown up for such a little lady. By the way, it's OK to forget his face and to go for long periods of time consumed with joy. You have to put his death in your heart and go on with the business of life. Anything else would be tragic. You belong to a special club; you have experienced great joy and deep sorrow at a very young age. Take those feelings and weave your life around them, you can make a difference. You should be proud of yourself. I know Bert is proud of you. You make us smile with your sweet and kind words of love and yes, of course we cry when we read your letters. We know you are one of the keepers of his soul, until we're all together again.

Now on to something fun. This year's Annual Deep Pit Barbecue extravaganza was better than ever. About a dozen of Bert's friends showed up, along with assorted camping gear and loaded down with bicycles. You could see them coming for at least a mile as their caravan of trucks on our old dirt road caused quite a dust storm. All were grinning, as they seemed to tumble and fall out of their trucks, excited that they finally arrived. They are such good friends and so close to one another. It hurts my heart to see them and know that they feel as we all do, still trying to deal with Bert's death. He was like their brother, they belong to the same club you do. We know that most of them will stay in our embrace forever, much like you!

I love who you are, Harriet

Harriet Bocca

January 1994

Hello dear Holly,

Hope your Christmas was beautiful and all that is good and wonderful surrounded you. As you know we always experience bitter sweet memories around the Holiday's. It's a far cry from when we had a house full of kids and all their friends. One thing I have learned is that life keeps evolving, nothing stays the same, and it shouldn't!

We're still traveling much of the year and it's been an eye opening experience. I get to explore quaint towns and ride my bike through every kind of situation imaginable. The coast of California is by far my favorite area. Crescent City, up by the Oregon border, has the most incredible coastline and the best little cheese factory ever. I think it's kind of a secret and off the beaten path. You can actually go on a self-guided tour and then, of course, eat plenty of free samples. Each morning Don goes to work and I get on my bike and meander around looking at all the nooks and crannies, which make up small towns. Many times I'll bring back some of the local fresh fish caught by one of the many independent commercial fishing boats, which arrive at the marina after a long day at sea. Sometimes I buy Smoked Salmon or pick wild blackberries as I ride along exploring. I must do a little bragging here, I've been known to make a pretty mean blackberry cobbler in our microwave with all the wild berries I find while on my bike! As you can tell, we make a home away from home, wherever we are. The list of interesting places and best place to eat, (tamales in Blythe, California) is endless. This month Don has organized an educational seminar in Ontario, California where we should be able to see old friends and family. I'm excited but don't think I'll find any wild berries!

Our place at Summer Lake is looking more and more like a campground. No hook ups, but we do have water when we run the generator and soon hope to have some solar panels to help. Little by little, we are improving our creature comforts. We now have a wooden structure, which we call an arbor but really looks like a chicken coop. However, it does provide some protection from the elements and makes our Labor Day Barbecue more comfortable for all, especially in the heat or wind.

Our grandchildren are all growing so fast, we know each moment is an opportunity to enjoy. Holly enjoy your opportunities with Nicolet and stay happy.

Love, Harriet

Harriet Bocca

Wild Blackberries Picked in Oregon

Words Spoken Only On Paper

February 1994

Dear Holly,

What a nice surprise I found in the mail when I returned home from our trip. How beautiful the wreath is, did you make it? The color is the same shade of rose that matches most of the accent colors in my house, so it is just perfect. Since we have a used brick fireplace that covers most of the living room wall, I will hang it alongside other decorations, which are hand crafted. What a thoughtful gift and best of all, it's a gift from you!

How is Nicolet doing? Let's see, she's most likely at the stage where she is sharper than a whip and keeping you really running. Are you still working? I know that the desert is busy this time of the year with all the sun seekers visiting, so your tips should be good.

Today I have my oldest granddaughter over to play, later we'll go pick up her big brother from school. Eloise will be five this week and her red hair reflects her personality. She really knows how to get into your heart and since she loves candy, I know how to get into her heart! She's so sweet yet aware and sensitive. Not long after Bert died she was playing dress up in the middle of the hallway and suddenly noticed the photos of all our children hanging on the wall. She recognized the high school photo of Bert and suddenly came running into the kitchen with her cheeks all flushed and so excited that she jumped up and down in delight! "Grandma, grandma, Uncle Bert's not dead, he's in the hallway, I can see him, you don't have to be sad anymore!"

    I was so sorry she felt my sadness, but it is part of the process. Do you remember how I told you that I write letters to my boys? Well, I'm still doing it, however I haven't re-read any of them. I just can't bear to, as most were written in anguish in the middle of the night, when sleep would not come or last. Oh Holly, some nights were never ending. The letters are powerful and spiritual as I write my most secret thoughts and unspoken words. It seems my relationship with them has changed, as now they are teaching me as I search for guidance. Some of the letters are surreal as they were raw with emotions and questions. I must admit, there are times when I feel they are still alive and this is all a horrific nightmare. Since I never had the chance to say good-bye to them, I continue to try to communicate through my letters. I believe they are closest to me when I sit at my desk and scribble words of longing and love. It's the isolated quiet moments, which are profound. At times it almost feels as if I have to allow the pain and terror of their deaths to sink in and wash all over me, for this nightmare and the overwhelming longing to be absorbed into my reality. This may be called an attempt to accept, however I know I will never accept, but I will adjust. People, who did not know our sons, can never know the loss. They can only imagine, have empathy, and reach out in kindness. Sometimes it's almost as if hearing that we have had two teenagers die is more than they can handle, uncomfortable in just what to say. I don't blame them; I don't know what to say! I only know that our boys had beautiful hearts and their warm wonderful natural kindness was like a magnet. They were given to us, and were ours to take care of, teach, and guide. My job was to give them birth, love them and care of them, I should have been able to protect them or prevent them from making bad choices, choices that cost them their lives. I should have done better.

Yesterday, I saw a neighbor who lives across the street greeting her adult son when he came by for a visit. He looked to be about the same age as our son Brandon, if he were still alive. I couldn't get over how much he reminded me of him, red hair and all. At least it was what I envision Brandon to look like at that age. This is something I do constantly in my effort to try to bring back my boys' images. This might be called a fantasy, as I hold onto this wonderful thought for just a split second. Similar to a dream, I pretend that my visitor at the front door is my son. Perhaps he would bring his wife and children along. This pause in reality makes my heart feel lighter, as if a heavy weight is lifted and bright sunlight enters my world. How I envied that neighbor whose son is real. I don't believe I am alone in these fancies, as most who have lost a loved one wish to have them back in their lives, even for one last visit or hug. These thoughts are with me all the time, yet tucked away safely. I miss the physical energy that teenagers have, and sometimes the loneliness creeps in, however I'm never lonely with these brief fantasies.

I didn't intend to get into this so deeply; it's just that I know you understand. It's an empty feeling in my heart and I can't fill it yet I know that I'm going on, because I have so many that need me. I actually laugh a lot and am fun to be around, honestly. It's just that I am always just a breath away from sorrow.

Harriet Bocca

Well, now that I've made your day, think I'll go out and play dolls with Eloise, or finish our art project. Thanks for being there; I know someday that we'll be able to be a more active part of each other's lives, perhaps we'll be neighbors, you never know!

With much love, Harriet and Bert, too. You make us smile!

March 1994

Harriet,

Been thinking a lot about you (and Bert) lately.

Nicolet is definitely two! She is pure sunshine to me, but I guess you know the feeling. So much has been happening; Tony and I have finally set the date for our wedding, June 11, this coming summer. We have grown together, he's a wonderful Daddy and easy to love.

I know Bert would be happy to know we are making the commitment and he would like my Tony now and the person he has become. Bert and Tony never got along, which was obvious, but Tony has changed. I know Bert loved me in a very special way and I feel I treated him badly; I'm so sorry about that. Tony said I should forgive myself and move on. Bert was such a special person I know he forgave me but it's hard for me to live with the guilt of hurting him.

All my love and thoughts, Holly

Dear Holly,

I've been carrying your beautiful letter with me for several days. I've longed for a quiet time by myself to be able to spend some time with you. I always do this with your letters, first I read them, and then I read them again, slowly!

You, my dear, must give yourself a break. Your Tony is so right, you need to forgive yourself and move on. I'm not saying forget, just put the past memories in a safe place and live the best happiest life you can.

I knew that you and Bert had broken up about the same time you got back together with your Tony. He told me all about it and that you remained the closest of friends, even when you were at odds with each other. True friends get through stuff like that and you did. I know

Harriet Bocca

that he would have wanted to be with you, but it was not to be. You already had someone very special in your life. How can you blame yourself? You were a good friend to him and you still are. How many mothers ever hear how sweet their sons were? You give me this gift every time you write. You confirm my knowledge that I did a good job in raising a son who was kind and giving. He was a son who did a lot of dumb ass things but still held to his true values and made a difference in our lives. We are not perfect and neither was he. Nevertheless, we learn, and he is helping us. He knows how you feel, and I'm proud that he had you in his life. He made a good choice in you.

Now you must move on to a fuller life. Your relationship with him will be a source of strength to you through the good and bad times. Let's make a deal? Let's be happy and joyful for the next fifty years. At the end of that time if we want we can sit down and reflect on all the sad times, but hey, we've got things to do! Time is ticking away, you've got a wedding to get ready for and a wonderful soon-to-be husband to care about. Nicolet needs a happy mommy. Be that happy mommy Holly, you deserve it.

I'm so glad that you and Tony are getting married. It means you are both ready to commit your lives together. I think Bert was right when he said that Tony wasn't good enough for you, I don't think he would have thought there was anyone good enough for you! However, now I think he would tell you both that your love has grown and you belong together.

Please send me an invitation, I know I won't be there but I will feel as if I am taking place in the bonding if I can hold your wedding invitation in my hands. I will be there in spirit, and delighted to know that you are happy and surrounded by loving people.

Yesterday is gone Holly, but there's a great big tomorrow!

Love, Harriet

August 1994

Dear Harriet,

Wow! I have so much to tell you, I don't know where to start. Definitely, the first thing has to be that by September 1st I will be living only a few hours away from Sacramento. We are moving to Susanville, California. It is not far from great fishing and camping. Tony is there already looking for a house and then Nicolet and I will join him as soon as possible. It's really beautiful up there, it reminds me of the area in the mountains where I was raised and have lived for so long. We're so excited about raising Nicolet in such a mountain community. First on my list is to tell you of our wedding,

It was a perfect day, so beautiful in many ways. All of Bert's friends showed up and were great. Tony was more or less an outsider with them, so it was really nice to see how much everyone has grown up and gotten along. Everyone had a lot of fun and old feelings were finally set aside. I will bring pictures to show you.

I think that the biggest change of all is me! I have been able to just step back and learn a lot about myself. I know that the three-year mark of Bert's death is coming up and I am still going to the cemetery, but I am a lot stronger this time. I know that the pain will never go away and it won't even get easier, but I have finally figured out that I can still miss him and be happy in my life at the same time. I still feel badly for the way I treated him, but I am confident in feeling that he definitely would have wanted me to be happy. I know he would want that for everyone! I know it will be a long time, or maybe even never, before I can completely be at peace with it or myself. But I have Nicolet to bring me so much happiness, how could I not accept that gift from her? You helped me to be strong and while I don't get the chance to see you, your letters are so encouraging. I automatically smile when I see one in the mailbox, before I even read it. Talk to you soon,

All my love, Holly

P.S. You make me Smile!

Dear Sweet Holly,

How very sweet of you to have shared in words, your wedding day. The maturity you have is remarkable, guess a lot has to do with the fact that you had to grow up fast. First you had to face the shock of the death of your best friend Bert and then to give birth to a baby. I know how the responsibilities that come with parenting can be overwhelming, especially when you're so young. It's so good to hear that so many of Bert's friends participated in your very special day. It was amazing when he died to have their awe-inspiring support. The days and nights following his death, many of them came to our house and stayed, sleeping on the floor as if to protect us. It was as if they needed us as much as we needed them. I hope you felt that power of

Harriet Bocca

support as you took your big step into a new life on your wedding day. That same bunch of now young adults has been there for us these last three years. Collectively they are strong, many of them have joined us at Summer Lake for our Deep Pit Barbecue; lending a hand whenever they could. I know they felt that they wanted to try to fill in where Bert would have been. It's really remarkable to see such friendship. Now you must realize that they are there for you too and wish only the best. Most of them are well on their way in life, but we know they will continue to stick together to support each other and that includes you and Tony!

It's been hot here in Sacramento, I ride my bike around the park every morning but by noon I'm ready for lunch and a nap. Oftentimes while eating lunch I will watch Andy Griffith's Mayberry on TV. It gives me hope that things are all good and life so simple. We've gotten into a routine, but still dream of building our little house up at Summer Lake. Our dream keeps us going and so do you.

Love, Harriet

September 1994

Dear Harriet,

Sorry that it has taken so long to get back to you, but I had a change of plans. Tony moved up to Susanville over a month ago and got a job on the second day, but just found a house a week ago! Therefore, I have been kind of floating around between family members in Southern California, waiting to move. I just got up here on the 10th and now live on the outskirts of this cute little town. It is so beautiful; my backyard is a great meadow and then trees forever. I definitely don't miss Southern California yet, except for my family, of course!

Sorry I couldn't make it to your barbecue this year, we will definitely be there next year for sure! I did get to spend some time in the mountains while I was waiting to move. Saw Bert's friends as well as Jimmy and the rest of the group. It was so much fun, I miss them, yet it's good to see that most are getting their stuff together, especially Jimmy who is going to EMT paramedic school and seems to have settled down.

Hope to see you soon. Maybe lunch or something? Thanks so much for all your letters, always makes me smile to see them in the mailbox!

All my love, Holly

Harriet Bocca

November 1994

Holly my dear,

I never told you how much I loved our short visit. It makes my heart feel happy to know you're happy and in such a loving relationship. I'm sorry I missed meeting Tony, he's such a lucky guy to have you in his life I know he must be special and he obviously loves Nicolet.

By the way, Larry called and wants your phone number; would you like me to give it to him? I know how he misses all of Bert's friends and finds it difficult staying connected. Since he and Ralph are going to Tahoe on winter school break, I've invited them to spend the night here on their way through. Both Don and I are proud that they have pursued their college education and have a positive eye on the future. The better each one of Bert's friends are, the better we are, which includes our dear sweet Holly.

Love and hugs, Harriet

December 1994

Dear Holly, Tony and Nicolet,

"LET IT SNOW, LET IT SNOW, LET IT SNOW!" Let me rephrase that, "LET IT SNOW," in the mountains, not here in

Words Spoken Only On Paper

Sacramento! I'm sure it's beautiful up there in the mountains as you gaze out your window and watch the beautiful perfect snowflakes fall and make everything clean and white. It takes a certain sturdy young soul to enjoy the aftermath of a heavy snowfall, but I believe you are a family that will love it and enjoy every moment.

We had planned to get up your way on our holiday visit to Summer Lake, however the predicted back-to-back winter storms for the Sierra's has caused us to rethink our plan. Our experience of traveling over the mountains in ice and snow is one thing, but to deal with all the holiday travelers (skiers) is a whole other ball game, and not always fun. We'll wait until after the holidays and for the first nice sunny weekend to make our trip. Our lemon trees are still loaded with juicy healthy lemons and I'll be sure and bring you a big bag. Perhaps I'll bring enough for you to share with friends. Who knows, maybe someone will bake a lemon meringue pie!

I hope your new job is working out well, Holly. I know how hard it is to work on weekends and not be at home with the family. Bet Tony enjoys seeing your smiling face when you walk in the door, after all, he's had his hands full being "house daddy" all day.

Do you have plenty of wood for the winter? If not, perhaps we could find a good resource for you; biggest problem would be the distance. I actually had a tree taken down in the backyard and had to pay to have the wood taken away. I don't think it was good firewood, but mixed with a hot hardwood fire and it might have been very usable.

Harriet Bocca

Keep happy and warm, may it be the best Christmas ever!

Love, Harriet and Don

January 1995

Dear Holly,

We arrived home late last night after driving for fourteen hours. Our trip to Southern California was fun and of course busy. Between Don's involvement with his seminar and visiting family, we crammed a whole lot of living into a very short time. My job at the seminar was to be the "gofer." I made twenty-four trips back and forth from our hotel room to our car in an effort to gather all the paperwork and electronic equipment needed. Now that doesn't sound right but it's true. Also had to drive to the airport and pick up a guest speaker who I didn't know nor did he know me, all we knew is where to meet. Unfortunately, he didn't have a cell phone so I took a chance and picked up the first good looking man I saw standing in front of the United Airlines baggage claim. Just kidding, but he was easy to spot since I got a flat tire on the way to the airport and by the time I arrived at the terminal there was just one man standing out front looking a bit lost. Of course, I did what any smart woman would do. I gave him the third degree, and offered him a ride! All worked out well and the seminar was a huge success. I'm proud of Don, he puts a lot of effort into promoting his industry and it's paying off.

We'll be leaving for Tampa on Friday, but I wanted you to know if by chance you do get down here for your concert please feel free to stay at our house. The key will be under the mat and I'll send you our daughter's phone number. She and her family live just five minutes away and she will be able to show you how to work the heater etc. if you have any problems. Our home is your home and the coffee will be ready to go, so enjoy.

We love you guys and are so sorry we will miss your time here in Sacramento.

Harriet and Don

Early Spring 1995

Dear Holly,

I started this letter while on the road, so I'll just blend the one I started with the rest.

Ukiah, California

I'm finally getting a chance to gather my thoughts and find some time to write.

We're about 70 miles North of San Francisco, watching it rain. According to the news on TV, Susanville should be getting some snow! Just think how beautiful it's going to be in a few weeks with all that moisture to green up everything. Before you know it summer will arrive and the lakes and rivers will be brimming. I'm so glad I had the chance to visit you and your little cabin in the woods. Now I know what your view is from your kitchen window. If I close my eyes, I see the meadow filled with snow surrounded by tall trees and a backdrop of snowcapped mountains. There you are, standing on your front porch with your long brown hair tucked under a knit cap. Little Nicolet is close by your side, all bundled up in layers of warm clothes to protect her from the cold. Your nose is red, yet you stay there enticed by the amazing view. I feel you are at peace with nature and hopefully yourself. Just think, soon your meadow will be filled with deep green grass and wild flowers. What a great place to live!

Yesterday Don and I had a little excitement when we found ourselves on a dirt road in a remote area. The road was filled with muddy deep potholes, thanks to the record-breaking rainfall. Don, in a macho mood, thought he could get through all the muck so he continued driving down the road, even though I voiced my concern! Sure enough, we got stuck and after two hours of trying to dig ourselves out (getting wet and muddy); we had to call a tow truck to rescue us. It was quite an afternoon and we were relieved to get back to the safety of our motel room, where we could shower and have a hot cup of soup.

I was so glad Don was not by himself, as he needed a cheerleader. Our relationship is to help one another. My part is to take care of him and keep our real life going, especially during the times we're away from home. I make a motel room feel like home in many ways. Our favorite blankets are placed at the foot of the bed as well as our own coffee mugs near the coffee pot, which is usually provided. Since most rooms come with refrigerators and microwaves, we often have "dinner for two" in our room. Sometimes I bring healthy frozen entrées and pick up a bag salad from the local supermarket. This way, after a hard long day at work, we can relax and get comfortable, just like home!

I must admit, traveling can be tiring and for me even some moments of boredom, since there is very little to do in a hotel or motel room. Obviously no house work, even if I do make the bed! Preparing dinner in a microwave occasionally is usually simple and easy to clean up. I'm usually left without transportation since Don takes the car and I'm left to my own resources. If I have my bike, I can ride to local places of interest, which is always fun and exciting. However, a motel room is a perfect place for me to write, with no interruptions.

As much as I love my man, he is quite a distraction! I've been fortunate that he has always respected my independence and encouraged me throughout our marriage. We are opposites in many areas of our lives, I'm the kind of person who gets to know the stranger sitting next to me on a plane, often times having deep and meaningful conversations, while Don is quite comfortable in his own space, without interruption. I love bright colors, and wind in my hair; he loves conservative colors and a controlled look. If we have bacon for breakfast he prefers it crispy, while you guessed it, I like it soft! I believe we have come together because of our differences…I bring excitement, he security. Our mutual philosophy's on politics, religion

Harriet Bocca

/spiritual and moral beliefs are one, yet as individuals, we can agree to disagree on specific issues. We truly have grown up together, and been very lucky that our paths have continued in the same direction. Don even likes chick-flicks! However, luck is just part of the equation; we've both had to learn to listen to each other. By the way, listening is a continual education program.

Back at home in Sacramento

Great news, the sun is finally out! I'll bet you're enjoying some nice weather too. I believe Northern California had record-breaking rainfall, so hopefully that means no drought this summer.

Last weekend we drove over the mountains to Summer Lake. We got all our pruning done and cleaned up from the last storm. I feel so good when I work in the dirt and the only distraction might be an occasional rabbit running through the sage brush. Do you know that rocks move all by themselves? It seems that every time I work out in the yard, I find more and more misplaced rocks. We saw about 40 deer grazing in our little experimental vineyard when we arrived, they must love the fresh new growth on the vines. Maybe they think they are helping me prune. Too bad, they like to dig up our irrigation system at the same time. It must be migration time for so many to be this close to people.

It was so good to see you a few weeks ago when I stopped in at your work place. You looked so cute with your uniform vest on and hair pulled back in a ponytail. Even though you were busy, you seemed to be in control and polite to each customer. There was a sense of peace about you as you worked with your customers. It's hard to believe you are so confident and mature, so different than the child I first met. You truly have bloomed into a complete woman. I wonder when that happened?

When are you going to come down to Sacramento again? Now that the weather has cleared up perhaps you will feel like taking a little trip out of town. We'd love to have you for Easter if you have no plans. Our daughter, her husband and two grandchildren will be here, so it should be fun. It would be great to meet your wonderful Tony.

Take care of yourself and we hope to see you soon.

Love, Harriet

Harriet Bocca

One of Our Friendly Rabbits

Words Spoken Only On Paper

August 1995

Dear Holly,

It's hard to believe that four years ago you gave me that beautiful bouquet of white roses and the sorrowful words of love included on the card. You must have gone through so much pain and I couldn't even help you. I barely could take care of myself; I still have a tough time taking care of me. It was truly a dark time for us all but we are getting better!

You have filled your life with such love. The birth of Nicolet must have been just what the doctor ordered as she has brought you to a higher level in your life plan. Tony seems to be good for you and you seem to be peaceful. Things happen for reasons we are not aware of, but if we open our eyes, we can understand. Actually if we open our hearts, we can understand!

In my quiet thoughts, I'm still sorrowful. However, I know that someday we will all be together and then all things will make sense, this is my mantra.

It was sad to hear of Jerry Garcia's death. I know you and Tony were fans of the Grateful Dead and his death was shocking to you. It was truly tragic, and I understand he struggled for such a long time to clean up his life and get off drugs. His talent and sensitivity seemed great. I'm not familiar with any specific songs that the Grateful Dead did, but I do remember hearing them in concert when we lived near CalExpo in Sacramento. I liked what I heard, and was surprised I didn't

Harriet Bocca

know much about them. However in the early 60's, when the Grateful Dead were just becoming known and popular, Don and I were newly married and having kids. Brandon the oldest, was born in 1962, Laurence, in 1964 and Anne in 1965, so we had our hands full. Then along came Bert in 1971. I was twenty-seven at that time and it was just like as if I had never been pregnant before because everyone was so excited. The children were eager at the prospect of a little brother to play with and Don even made me a few outfits to wear for my pregnancy. I failed to mention to you that he actually likes to sew, since his mother was a professional tailor and he picked up the talent when he was just a little boy. When I conceived Bert, it was a lunchtime quickie, which I remember well. It seems like those years are a blur since Don and I were struggling and had our hands full being parents. Our primary goal was to take care of our family and meet our responsibility. We were more into Little League and PTA and never seemed to have time to pay much attention to the popular music or movements. However now that we've got the time I'm seriously considering going in that direction and catching up with all the stuff we missed.

Speaking of the Grateful Dead, did Bert ever tell you about his Italian burrito concession at their concert here at CalExpo? He made spaghetti with red sauce, added garlic, onions, and cheese and wrapped them in flower tortillas. He road my bike to the fairgrounds and sold them for $1.00. I don't think he made much money but quite a few "Dead Heads" had a good high carbohydrate meal! He did meet up with Toby, (an old friend from the mountain), who was a Grateful Dead fan. Toby had a neat Volkswagen bus, one you would have loved and they hung out during the concert. Bert was always making new friends, or finding old ones. This all seems like a million years ago.

If you make it to our Annual Barbecue at Summer Lake, be sure and bring some of their tunes. By the way, Christine, Steve's mom will be there. Since she and Steve were so close to Bert they have reached out to us, she becoming our rock when the winds of life blew too hard. Christine will bring her bike and we plan on riding down the road, in search of a special place, I call the Angels Meeting Place. It's where I have witnessed strange and beautiful visions during dramatic weather changes in our valley and over the mountains. It reminds me of familiar pictures of angels rising up and flapping their wings in unison. The first time I experienced this spectacular event I was sitting in front of our trailer watching a massive powerful storm build as it developed on the very tops of the Sierras. The elevation of the gigantic granite peaks are well over 10,000 feet and the cool moist air from the Pacific Ocean flows across the interior of California slamming into these mountains. The power of the wind hits the solid wall causing an eruption of cool air to collide with the dry hot air of the eastern side of the slopes. This mixture of hot and cold air creates turbulence with sometimes gale force winds as it pulls the moisture up and over. Here is where I vision the angels as they maneuver quite gracefully through the eye of the storm.

If you do come on Labor Day, I'll put in a request to see what can be done to give us a show! I know Christine would love to get to know you better and together we would feel privileged if you joined us on our personal journey. Our route will be to head across the valley,

Harriet Bocca

due west, riding with the sun in our eyes as we search for the big meadow. Perhaps we'll find the angels warming up their wings as they await the arrival of the storm. I wonder if the warm wind helps them take flight. Who knows, we might even follow a rainbow and find a pot of gold! We can always dream.

I love you and your sweetness,

Harriet

May 1996

Dear Holly,

I hope by now you are settled in your new home and have found it comfortable and cozy for your family. I tried calling you and reached your machine, so hope you got my message. I know it's never easy moving, but I bet you're more organized than I.

Did I ever tell you that I believe that you are an old soul, one who has purpose and wisdom? You are very astute for a woman so young. The very moment I need reassurance and comfort I seem to hear from you, it's as if I'm lost and you reach out to help me find my way home. By the way, my vision of me being lost is of a face darting from one person to another looking for someone or something familiar. It's a frantic feeling and one which makes me feel uneasy and alone. Just when I'm drowning, going down for the third time, you reach out and save me. Your recent letter and beautiful angel pin arrived just in time. How did you know I needed you? I've placed the angel on my writing desk, where she can watch over me. Thank you for being you and such a beautiful angel.

This August we are going to be in Southern California for work. I'm planning on having a little memorial for Bert and Brandon. Since both boys died on the mountain, I thought it might be nice to hold the ceremony near the nature trail where they spent many hours hiking. I hope you will be able to get there. Since the handmade angels you sent me were so unique, I was wondering if you might be able to make some for those who will be participating, I love the simplicity of your little angel and know that others will think them special too.

Today, we're in a small community north of Paso Robles on Hwy 101 in Central California. It's a quiet farming community with plenty of neighborhood roads to ride my bike and lots of friendly people. Traveling is always fun as it's such an opportunity to see how people live, and it helps me understand that people are basically the same.

Harriet Bocca

An Angel from Holly

Words Spoken Only On Paper

Did I tell you that Darrell was over at Easter time? He had a rough time when Bert died, but finally got his act together and went on to college. He even has a summer job as an apprentice for an architectural firm in San Jose, California. In the fall, he'll go back to school and graduate next spring. He once told me that when he rides his bike, he knows Bert is with him, encouraging him to keep going in life. I think he's on the right track. I know his family is very proud of him and so are we. It's amazing how many of Bert's friends have picked up the pieces after his death and gone on with their lives in a productive way. When I think of how many have gotten married, had children and become responsible adults, I'm impressed. Some have gone on to further their education and even one joined the peace core, making a difference in this big wide world. Yet for the most part they have remained as close as ever, much like brothers and sisters.

Got a lot going on with my grandchildren this week; we're going to plant a garden. They are growing too fast, I'm sure your Nicolet is too.

Take care my dear sweet Holly. Hug your family close.

Love, Harriet

I received a beautiful thank you card for a gift certificate at a craft store I had sent Holly. I knew how much she enjoyed making crafts.

Harriet Bocca

June 1996

Dear Holly,

It was great hearing from you. I'm so excited to hear of your plans to move to Oregon. We've been up there many times and can never seem to get enough of all the green trees and have great memories of picking wild berries. You seem to be seeking a more natural way to live, one that you are comfortable with and that fits your lifestyle. You have learned something which many never learn; to live and do what you love. All the rest will fall into place as you find your happiness.

Thank you for agreeing to make your sweet little angels for our "Walk in the Forest a Time to Remember." They will be appreciated and a nice remembrance of the day. We expect about thirty people to attend and the angels will be a remembrance for all.

Saw Darrell last week and he has a chance to intern for a global marketing business this summer. How exciting for him, this just might be the "proverbial foot in the door." The opportunity to learn and perhaps travel for a company worldwide right out of college must be a dream come true.

Hope to see you at our get together, we'll keep our fingers crossed.

Love, Harriet

Words Spoken Only On Paper

August 1996

Dear Holly, Tony and little Nicolet,

It was so good to see you last week; you helped make the evening special for us all. I am so amazed and impressed with how you and Tony have evolved in your relationship. It's obvious that your deep love and commitment are truly what a relationship should be about. You teach by your example. This doesn't surprise me at all, as you have always possessed a special sensitivity which most have neglected to develop in their lives.

I wanted to thank you again for the beautiful "Holly Angels." They were appreciated as I handed them out at our gathering. I know those who received one will always think of the special time we all shared together. I have mailed one to my sister, who along with many family members, shares our grief. I will send one to Gabby, who is now working in Zimbabwe for the Peace Corps and one to her mother in Utah; both angels themselves. If I can talk you into making some more I would be able to share them with the people I meet who need something to hang onto when they are faced with trauma and fear.

I remember all too well my need to hang onto something after our boys died, especially after Bert died since I was away from family and support. After his funeral, we had to make the long trip back to Sacramento and it was very isolating. We had not lived there long and I knew very few people. That trip was hell and when I walked in our apartment, which Bert had shared with us for a short time, I panicked!

Harriet Bocca

The only thing I could do was clutch the cards and letters, which we received from loved ones. Your card was on top of the pile and the moment I read it, I knew by your words that our pain was our bond. The other powerful thread of support came from the telephone book. Somehow, I had the wherewithal to seek help from a professional, but not knowing who that would be I fumbled through the yellow pages and found community support groups. As tears fell on the pages and uncontrolled sobs took control of my whole body I saw the words, Compassionate Friends. It was described as support group for parents who have lost a child and there was a twenty-four hour hot line. Oh, that poor woman who answered my call, she was so calm and understanding and I was so incoherent and terrified. That one call may have saved my life. It was validation that I was not alone; I was not the only mother who had two children die. I would survive.

Through my experience, I understand so well the feeling of hopelessness and immediate terror death can bring to loved ones. Perhaps that's why I feel confident in working in the grief field. Your little angels will be the perfect gift I can give to someone who is in the throes of such a traumatic experience. They will recognize that your angels were made with love.

Words Spoken Only On Paper

A poem to dear Holly

August 1996

She came into his life so sweet and kind.

Theirs was a special soul bond and now it's mine.

Her heart was broken when he left us so fast.

But her love as ours was the kind that lasts.

I will hold her so close when she might show doubt,

yet will let her go free to fly all about.

Although she will grow gracefully into a lighthearted soul,

our bond will remain solid and never grow old.

How special he was to gather her into his life

for he knew I would need her but not as his wife.

Their kind of love was different indeed a more

sensitive and sincere act which was more than most need.

As I grasp for some knowledge of what more there could be

Harriet Bocca

I know that she is there and it's so easy to see.

That love is forever as we move about

jumping from place to place without a thought or a doubt.

We cannot change our path or direction

only embrace each other in this life's selection.

So enjoy and experience each new day,

hug your family and fly away.

To a place we all came from and a place we must go

because life's just a stopping place this we all know.

Love Always, Harriet

Holly's plans to move to Oregon were delayed and she and her family moved back to her hometown until they could make more permanent plans.

Words Spoken Only On Paper

March 1997

Dear Harriet,

    Greetings, and salutations, I had to sit down and drop you a note because I have been thinking about you for a month now. Hope you and Don are enjoying life. Things are good her, Nicolet, is enjoying being five and already talking about six!

    We relocated back to our old neighborhood in the mountains. Tony has found a job in the valley but hates it; I try to stay on the mountain where it's cooler and more trees. I want to plant a garden, but I have the feeling change is coming, maybe a move. (I hope so)

    We don't want to get stuck here, but we're glad we came. We think we will probably go back to Susanville, how silly is that? It's hard to go see all the places you think you would like to live in, guess it's just a process of elimination! I really miss the nature of the Sierra Nevada's and we were so lucky to make so many kind friends. I don't miss the tourists though. We'll just have to wait and see I guess.

Harriet Bocca

I love you, Holly

PS Did you guys get to check out the comet Halle Bopp? Awesome

April 1997

Dear Harriet,

    I have recently started going to the gym at 6:00 am, there I connected with Jessie, who married Bert's good friend, Jeremy. It's been great to see her again. We have been talking about you and what an amazing person you are.

    I want to make sure that you know how much you mean to me. You once told me that you thought Steve's mom was an angel, well I think that of you. Maybe everyone has someone like that, I believe you are mine. You have no idea what you have done for me as a person, as a woman, and especially as a mother. You really have given me so much strength and I wanted you to know how much it means to me. I feel so blessed that I have been given such a special friendship with you and that God lets me know so many amazing people, including Bert. Especially Bert! Did you know how giving the two of you are? That is the best word I could ever use to describe you both. I have been with him many times since he has been gone. Someday I would really like it if we could sit and have tea and I could tell you about it. I have had a handful, a treasured handful, of these experiences and always I am left feeling so blessed to have known him and of knowing you as the outcome. People say that when young people die, "he didn't have a chance to live or he had so much to give, what a shame." But even in his short time here he gave so much and changed so many people's lives forever. I know he was just a gift; a gift giver is my name for him, and you too. I hope that this letter is not making you sad, that would make me feel so bad. These things don't make me sad anymore, they make me really happy and mostly thankful. You should be so proud! Even though I know you because of him, you have been more to me for a long time than just his mother. I wish I could put into words all that

Harriet Bocca

you have given me; I don't have those words through, but I can take this opportunity to tell you that I love you and every time I think of you my heart smiles.

With love, Holly

May 1997

Dear Holly,

    Today is our 35th wedding anniversary and I received one of the most beautiful gifts a person could receive, a letter from you! It was so special and sensitive, I am awed by your ability to reach out and touch me when I need you most. How could I have been so lucky to have a son who knew that I would need someone like you? You have helped fill the hole in my heart.

    I believe I told you that you are the only girl he ever wanted me to meet and get to know! I understand what you are saying when you talk of being with Bert, as both he and Brandon are with me always. Sometimes my internal conversations with them are as if we are in the same room and I feel a certain comfort in their presence. Right after Brandon died in 1980; I would get up each morning and have a cup of coffee with him. I had his picture on the mantel, and there I would sit, as if he were there. It was so comforting to have our little visit, when the house was quiet and still. After Bert died, I stopped my intimate visits with Brandon; it was as if I knew the boys were together! I know this sounds strange, but I had the feeling that it took a few weeks for them to connect. This is how I perceive the process and now they will be together forever. Perhaps that is why they died, they had a job to do, dying, and leaving us was part of their job. Perhaps writing to you and giving voice to my feelings is part of my job.

Now they are helping each other with the mission they were assigned to accomplish. I can now talk with them easily as they are very close. Bert is always close to you too. I believe you two have been together before. Our humanness gets in the way of our true spirit, but we can feel their power, if we only listen carefully. Once when we visited I told you that I don't know where Bert came from; because I don't believe he has been in my life before. That must sound strange, but he was different.

While it gives me great comfort to know my boys are so close, I do suffer from moments of selfishness and self-pity. It has also been a time of great growth for me, and I know that this life experience is something that I must use to accomplish the things which I am here to carry out. I also know that I will never stop being their mom.

Yes, dear Holly, your letter brought tears to me, but they were good tears, as we all need to be able to let the tears flow. As you know all too well, sometimes we just have to let our feelings happen and get them out!

Harriet Bocca

Don and I will be going to our place in Summer Lake tomorrow and spend about a week. We'll be planting quite a few trees, which we've established here in pots in Sacramento. Our property up there is beginning to look inviting now that we have things growing and our water system worked out, but I'm getting anxious to build a little farm house. Since we're both getting older, we need to get something built up there so we have time to enjoy it.

I'm excited to hear you are considering moving back to Susanville, as you'll be much closer to us. There are many neat places to live in the Sierra's, I'm sure you'll find your place.

Words Spoken Only On Paper

35 Tears of Growing in Love

Harriet Bocca

We'll be celebrating our anniversary on Labor Day, since so many friends and family attend our annual barbecue. I actually bought an old-fashioned antique lace long dress. I'll accessorize with work boots and a straw hat! Classy aren't I? Don plans to put on his red suspenders, cowboy hat, and shorts. We'll stand under our windmill and hopefully our grandchildren will carry desert wildflowers. It would be great if you could make it, but we understand about your need to take care of your personal business there on the mountain. I know moving can be a big job as well as an emotional one, but well worth it when your move brings you peace and happiness. Remember, if you can dream it, you can do it!

I love you, Harriet

August 1997

Dear Holly and family,

I thought you might enjoy a copy of our, "Growing in Love" a tribute written for our 35th anniversary. I plan to read it at our gathering. Don will have to improvise, since he's not the wordy kind of person and it's not his thing to show emotion, at least not in front of others; typical guy.

Take care of yourself and family, dear Holly.

Love, Harriet

Words Spoken Only On Paper

35 Years of Growing in Love

Actions Speak Louder Than Words

1962 - 1997

Thirty-five years ago, two seventeen year olds were cruising down Brand Boulevard in the San Fernando Valley. It was a time in American history when life was much simpler and safer. Mothers stayed home with the kids, divorce was considered a shame, and families actually had dinner together! On this particular hot summer night, something special was about to happen. The two somewhat naive teenagers were about to have a chance encounter, this event would change their lives forever!

The boy had his hair styled in a crew cut, a hairstyle popular in the early sixties. He was somewhat shy and still fighting adolescent pimples. He thought he looked cool driving his Dad's 1957 red pickup truck wearing dark sunglasses at night! The girl was a really cute blond, even if it did come from a bottle. She had borrowed her parents' car for the evening and along with her girlfriend they were listening to the radio playing Richie Valens' "La Bamba" as they cruised down the street!

It was a magical night as his truck came to an easy stop alongside the girls' car. He had spotted them a few blocks back and had been weaving his way in and out of traffic trying to catch up with them. He knew they must have been from the local Catholic high school, as

Harriet Bocca

he had never seen them at his school, San Fernando High. Although there were plenty of cute girls on his campus, this girl was definitely different! That night she caught his eye, and his heart! The one thing this unsuspecting boy didn't know, was that this girl had always believed that she would meet and marry a boy who had a red pickup truck! He didn't have a chance!

Little did the two know just how important that meeting was going to be. It would be the start of something big! The odds were against them, but their love, or should I say lust, was strong, (remember they were seventeen)! They didn't just fall in love, they grew in love!

We stand before you today, as a testimony of that growth and love. As the years seemed to have passed at lightning speed, the wishes for ourselves have turned into wishes for others. We have fulfilled many our dreams and the ones we couldn't we must accept. We are partners in life; and we have evolved into better. Our commitment has sustained us through the years, thanks to the support and love of family and friends. Together we have learned to hold each other, at the tender moments, as well as hold each other in moments of anger, hurt, fear and the countless other emotions we humans experience. Our marriage has not always been perfect; at times, we simply held each other up to keep from falling. We have experienced the greatest joys, as well as the greatest sorrow. Yet we are still one. Remember: It's not what you say to each other as much as what you do. Actions do speak louder than words!

Love, Harriet and Don

Words Spoken Only On Paper

Holly, as you know we are following our dream, so within the next few years we will be building our "little house on the prairie" at Summer Lake. We'll have no utilities, so it will be mostly solar, well water and Don has even promised to build an outhouse. What more could a girl want?

I must admit I have some doubts about the thought of living so far away from civilization, and such a different life style. I'll probably make friends with the local sheepherder, as they seem so friendly! As our dream becomes more of a reality, I try to imagine how life will be on the "prairie." Don, in his ever-wise and courageous attitude gently tells me, "it should be no problem," and explains how we'll have all the modern conveniences we've grown accustomed too. He confidently tells me, we'll adjust, then he repeats his all- time favorite two words, "Trust me!" Well Holly, I've trusted him for 35 years guess I can trust him another 35!

Harriet Bocca

January 1998

Dear Harriet,

Hello! Let me start by saying thank you for the Christmas gifts. I absolutely loved your New Year's letter; you make me laugh and cry at the same time. You are such a thoughtful person, you truly help inspire the way I live my life.

I sort of lost my mind for the month of December, but am feeling much better now. I got rear-ended in early December and hurt my back and neck. Once a week I go to physical therapy. To top it off, my VW bus was totaled. I'm still upset about it, but overall, I had an angel with me that day and I'm so thankful.

Nicolet turned six this month and had her first birthday party. She had so much fun, me too! She lost her first tooth a week later. My older sister moved up here on the mountain in December with her husband and my niece and nephew. We've all been having lots of fun; it's good to have her so close.

Words Spoken Only On Paper

Mainly, Tony and I are excited about our decision to move to Idaho sometime in June, when the weather is nicer. We're trying to be patient, but part of us has already left. I am thrilled to move on to this part of our life, and to see Nicolet grow up in such a special place. I look forward to the change and the growth such a rural mountainous area will bring us all, it will be a life changing adventure and one we welcome.

I loved your Anniversary picture and your letter telling about you and Don's dream of building in the wide-open spaces high in the Sierra Nevada. I think it's just wonderful and know you will be just fine living without all the modern conveniences you are used to. A satisfaction comes with being able to live without them and relying on yourself and each other. The rewards will make you forget why you ever needed them to start with!

I have wanted to tell you that when I was done reading your letter, I couldn't help but to think of Bert, and how proud he would be of your whole family, especially you! I know how

Harriet Bocca

hard it has been; you are so strong. I love you so much and hope to get to chat with you soon.

All my love, Holly

February 1968

Dear sweet Holly,

What a beautiful picture of "big girl" Nicolet you sent. Her eyes are just like yours. It's amazing how fast they grow and it seems she's growing into a beautiful young lady right before our eyes. In the photo, I see what looks like a new bike. I'll bet she loves it and I'll bet you are nervous about her riding, it's a mom thing.

I am sorry to hear about your accident and glad to know you were not injured any worse than you were. It's better to have your VW totaled than you, but I understand how upset you must be seeing your pride and joy all smashed up. Keep up with your physical therapy as it can work wonders. I hope you have a fair and timely settlement and that the insurance companies don't drag it out. Sometimes fighting for your rights can be just as exhausting and stressful as the accident itself.

Your dream to move to Idaho sounds so right for all of you. I know how much your passion for life is in the beauty of nature. Your strong spirit needs to be in a natural place. You have had a tremendous impact on me and how I think about things more organic and real.

We're here in Portland, Oregon for the entire week. While Don's teaching at a seminar I'll try to look up Bert's good friend, Phillip. I know he works in the area and we have sort of lost track of him. I've left a few messages on his answering machine, but so far no word.

Next day, Phillip called back and he dropped by after work. He looks just the way he did as a young teenager who called our family his. He was always the lost one, but I'm happy to say he seems to be doing great. He has a job he seems to love and apparently has a nice girlfriend who keeps him out of trouble. I've always said, "Every boy needs a good woman to help him become a man!" We went out to dinner and he came back to our room and watched the Olympics on TV. Don stretched out on the bed and Phillip on the couch, in less than an hour they were both asleep. Just like when he was a teenager sleeping on our couch, he never seemed to want to go home.

Thank you for being you.

Love, Harriet

Harriet Bocca

April 1998

Dear Holly,

How very sweet and so much like you to send the darling little craft angel and angel journal book. I save and treasure everything you have sent me through the years and have quite a nice collection of Holly treasures all through the house.

I've been busy with granddaughters this last week, as they are here on a visit. The picture you sent of Nicolet is so cute and she is about the same age as our granddaughters. What a handful of energy and fun. Perhaps someday they will all get together.

I'm excited to hear your plans on moving are going forward, and getting close! I feel a little sad that you will be going so far away, but know that it's your dream. We all must follow our dreams. We can always keep in touch via postage, phone, and even email. We're still working on our plan of building a little house in the wild. I'm mentally and physically getting rid of stuff, so our move will be easier.

Got an email from Darrell with the good news; he's graduating from college next month. It took him longer than planned, as he had to secure scholarships to help his finances. What an accomplishment, he struggled for such a long time, but stuck with it. Needless to say, we're so very proud of him, it's as if he were our own. We plan to attend his graduation and help celebrate his success. He's been offered a job with a southern California company based out of San Diego. Part of his work will require traveling all over the world. Now how can a young man pass up that opportunity? We also saw Toby in Seattle, Washington last month. As you may remember, he was the one who moved around a lot, always looking for a family to call his own. I know that when Bert died he had a bad time, but didn't we all. He's not changed at all, still dreaming of becoming an actor, still driving that old beaten- up truck. Just like in the old days, he is looking for someone to love him and bring out the best in him. Guess he needs a good woman!

Grandkids are calling, so time to get going. We're off to the Nature Center here in Sacramento to take a walk on the wild side. The girls will love it and so will I.

Please take care of yourself, and be happy! You have been a bright light, in my world of many colors.

All my love, Harriet

Harriet Bocca

September 1998

Dear Harriet,

We finally made our move to Idaho! I wanted to write you sooner, but have been so busy. I have a little part-time job at a really cute shop in town, so I have sort of re-entered society, but I am still dealing with my injuries from my car accident.

Nicolet has started first grade and loves it! There are 14 first graders in her school and a total of 150 K-9 students. I feel like I have always lived here. I felt like that the very first time I came to this beautiful area. It's so peaceful and quiet and all I hoped it would be. I feel blessed in many ways!

Jessie and Jeremy called the day after their wedding. Jessie and I have become close since Bert died. They were thrilled that you and Don were able to attend, it meant a lot to them. I am so excited for them, they seem so happy.

Words Spoken Only On Paper

I'm glad we had that conversation on the phone regarding my relationship with Bert and how Tony feels about it. He knows that I loved Bert very much, but not in the way I love him, yet it has been a struggle for both of us to make peace with those feelings. Bert died so young. He was always a gentleman and a good person. He had the best soul and I know I will be touched and changed forever for knowing him.

All my love, Holly

October 1998

Dear Holly,

    It was wonderful hearing from you as you have been on my mind. The weather must be turning cold up there and no doubt, you're getting ready for winter. I'm glad that things are going well as you settle into your new life in the high mountains. Thank you so much for sending the little book on friends. How very like you to have presented me with such a treasure.

    Thought you would like to know that in a recent conversation with Darrell, he told me that Bert had so much respect for you and that everyone knew your friendship was extraordinary and a one of a kind. By the way, your love for your husband Tony is so obvious, and your protection of his feelings beautiful. By nature, you are a kind and loving person and he must be proud of you for that attribute. He's one lucky man, who deserves a wonderful woman like you.

It sounds like you've found your dream in Idaho. It's funny how we as humans connect to something or someone so easily. We get that familiar feeling of comfort as if our search is over. Do you believe in reincarnation? This has intrigued me most of my life. I've always felt that I lived in the high deserts and was a pioneer woman. There's a lot written about past lives but obviously no proof, somewhat like God, a lot written but no proof! The thought of reincarnation is compelling to me, as it may explain my comfort in the high desert. I actually can vision myself as a young girl in a small cabin and my mom cooking on a wood stove.

Do you remember when you moved to Susanville? It caused me concern as I had always felt that I had been there in another life, as an early pioneer woman. Life was tough, but then I realized for you that it would be much different, as you would have all the modern conveniences, such as four-wheel drive.

We'll be putting our house here in Sacramento up for sale this spring. Our plans to build our "little house on the prairie" at Summer Lake in the high desert of Nevada are coming along well. We hope to have the foundation dug, forms and concrete poured and complete the basement by summer. Our biggest obstacle is one of money, as we plan to pay cash for everything. We're getting too old to take on financial burdens, especially now that Don has started his own consulting company. Being in business for yourself can be rewarding, however it's risky not knowing what your income will be from month to month. If all goes well we'll have a "barn raising" party at our next year's Annual Barbecue. Our hope is to have the house all sealed up before the winter snow hits. We'll need all the extra help from those who attend our get together, to help make that happen. Otherwise, we'll live in our travel trailer until the house is acceptable to our standards. Considering my past life experiences, I should be happy with a roof over my head and a warm fire to keep warm. Since we will be totally self-sufficient and rely on the use of solar power for electricity, we have our work cut out for us. It's a good thing Don is smart enough to figure the solar out and also build a house. As long as he's confident that this will work; I'm confident. It's also a good thing that we have so many supportive friends and family. I'm not sure they really realize what they are getting themselves into, but hey, we'll feed them.

It's good to hear that you've gotten a part time job, as it's fun to meet new people and feel like you're contributing. Not that being a wife and mother isn't a full time job; it's always good to get out and about. I'm sorry you're still in pain from your accident; I know it can be tiring and depressing to live in pain. Please take care of yourself, as you know your family needs you. I hope Tony is working steadily and enjoying his new job. I'll bet you're both busy getting wood in for the long winter, which is soon approaching. How neat to spend Christmas in such a winter wonderland. Do you have a wood stove or fireplace? We're planning on a wood stove for our little house and it will be the only heat we will rely on. While the snowfall isn't that much at Summer Lake, the temperature can drop way down to the teens, and every once in a while get below zero! That's plenty cold enough for us!

I'm glad you talked with Jessie and Jeremy. Attending their wedding was an emotional event for us, knowing we would see so many of Bert's closest friends. While we have stayed in touch through the years, we haven't actually seen a number of them in person since the funeral. Did you know that Bert was instrumental in Jessie and Jeremy getting together? I'm sure he would have been a big part of the wedding and it would have been a celebration he would not have wanted to miss. It was touching at times as we visited with Bert's friends, catching up with all the news and seeing so many who were once teenagers and now adults. I must admit I was momentarily envious of the bride and groom's parents, as they stood there and witnessed the happy event. I wished Don and I could experience that happiness. I guess you could say I had a silent pity party! This is how it is when I receive invitations and announcements from any of his friends. While I'm happy that they have moved on and continued their lives, I also feel a stab of pain for what we have lost and will never have. Please understand that I would not have wanted to miss any of their happy events!

I hope Nicolet enjoys her new school, what an experience to live in such a small community. I'll be thinking of you this winter, and know that you are OK as long as you have each other.

Love, Harriet

December 1998

Dear Harriet,

    Thanks so much for the Christmas gifts, you are always thoughtful. This is our first Christmas with just the three of us, we went snowboarding. I am so glad to hear about your move to Nevada. I will write you a real letter soon, but I just wanted to say thanks.

Love, Holly

February 1999

Dear Harriet,

    You are never far from my thoughts and I knew I must write. I hope all is well with you and your family. Things are outstanding with us here in Idaho. While there's not much money to be made, it's a fantastic way of life! We truly love it here.

    When will you be making the move to Nevada? I don't know if I told you that I spent every summer at Summer Lake, from age six to sixteen. I have wonderful memories of the area and camping. I'm very excited for you and Don and wish you happiness as you pursue your dreams. Following your heart is good for your soul!

    Nicolet seems to double in size every moment, and I try to soak up all of her. I love the person she is becoming, she is the greatest thing I ever did. She has adjusted to the move well and has lots of friends. She joined gymnastics and is involved in 4H, which is a big deal here. Tony's grandparents are moving up here in April and we're really excited to have them so close. Both Tony and Nicolet are the sun and moon to them. I was in California last month for a week and traveled up the mountain to see Jessie and Jeremy's new house they just built. Jessie is so cute and loves being married. I got a chance to visit with Jimmy as well. He looks good and happy now that he has a new girlfriend, who he really seems to care for. I think his heart is beginning to heal itself. It has taken him a long time to get over Bert's death, you know how he looked up to him as a big brother.

    I talked to Bert about a month ago in a dream. Do you dream about him? I'm sure you do! I feel so lucky when he is in one of my dreams, happy to see his face again, but always sad when I wake up and he's gone. Even though I am twenty-five now, he still seems to be wiser than I am. I hope you don't think I am selfish to talk to you about him, I believe he wanted us to be friends. I will always be connected to him, through you. It is funny how much time can go by, but missing knowing him, never lessons. I think that it may even grow. He is such a big part of who I am and who I want to be. You must have been an amazing mother when he was a boy; he continues to be the most pure hearted, beautiful person I have ever known. You inspire me to do the same for Nicolet, and he inspires me in so many ways, but mostly to live and see and feel, and never miss a moment.

    I hope that I have not made you too sad; it makes me happy to think of him. I hope we will

Harriet Bocca

both be still enough to speak soon, be happy and have fun.

Love, Holly

March 1999

Dear Holly,

    Your letter was such a beautiful gift and one I will add to the many you have given me through the years. I know Bert gave you me in order to help share the pain of his physical absence. However, as you point out so beautifully he is with us in spirit in even a stronger and more profound way.

    Your life sounds peaceful and your personal growth to be admired. You've always recognized the need for your soul to be in a quiet setting which gives you opportunity to grow and know. How lucky Tony and Nicolet are to have you in their lives, as I know you are a teacher.

    We are getting excited about living in Nevada at Summer Lake and away from it all. It's kind of scary thinking about all the changes but stimulating at the same time. I guess you experienced that same feeling when you made the move to Idaho. In your heart you know it's good but being so far away from loved ones is hard. It's good to hear that Tony's grandparents will be living near you, as they will enrich your life and add much to Nicolet's growth. We grandparents are good to have around. By the way, I think 4H is the greatest organization. The program teaches understanding, responsibility and commitment at an early age, good for little Nicolet!

I've enclosed a video of Jerry Garcia. When I saw that it was going to be on TV I knew I needed to tape it for you. He seemed to be such a loving inspirational man to many yet could not control his human need to self-indulge. If only he could have touched the souls of man without having to retreat to drugs to sustain his creative talent. Perhaps we would have never heard and experienced such a sensitive soul had he not given himself permission to self-destruct. Perhaps that was his purpose and through his pain, others have gained.

Tonight I start assisting in a program through Hospice that helps children overcome grief and loss. It's called Children's Bereavement Art Group (CBAG) and I'm looking forward to learning about how to help children through difficulties. Some of the children will be referred by the courts, others requested by their family. We'll work with watercolors tonight and in the ten- week course the children will learn how to express themselves through art. One project will be a grief mask they will make from clay. Since I will be working directly under an art therapist, I hope to learn quite a lot from her. They say that this type of grief work helps give children a vocabulary, a voice, to express themselves in a safe non- judgmental place. I believe adults can benefit from this type of therapy as well. We adults may have the vocabulary to express our grief, but tend to edit ourselves, so we don't sound uncontrolled. Adults are far too aware of judgment. Children

Harriet Bocca

seem to be more open and honest unless they have learned to disguise their true feelings. This is the difficult part as they will hold in their grief and it may manifest in other ways such as anger, acting out, discipline and on and on. If not dealt with and the child unable to express their feelings, ask questions or talk about fears they will carry it far too long.

As you know, I have been writing articles about grief and loss. It's my way to work on my sorrow and try to make sense out of the death of two beautiful amazing sons. Therefore, writing is my therapy, my retreat and a place to validate their lives. I hope that my work can also help others. I've recently submitted a short story for publication, I know it will help people understand that they are not alone in their silent thoughts. I certainty have become a better person as I've traveled through this wilderness and hopefully more sensitive to others. Perhaps like Jerry Garcia we all have had to go through the pain, so that others and we can gain.

Be happy dear Holly and enjoy your life as never before!

P.S. We're working on our house here in Sacramento, painting and cleaning in hopes that we'll be able to sell by summer and continue on our dream to move up to Summer Lake. I do believe timing is everything in life and now is the time for us to make the move.

Love, Harriet

Words Spoken Only On Paper

June 1999

Dear Holly,

 Hope this short letter finds you as happy as can be and that your winter was mild and fun with just enough sun.

 Our house is now officially up for sale, obviously, we are excited. Don was busy researching online this last winter to find out all he could on how to build a solar home. It's not quite like a regular house, since we have to plan on storage for a number of very large batteries which will store the power we make during the day when the sun is out. Then there's a lot of technical stuff, which I don't really understand but that's why I have Don! He made multiple trips these past few months to Summer Lake getting things ready. He had to coordinate the concrete contractor and see that the excavating was done correctly for the daylight basement, which is part of the foundation. All this work has to be completed by summer. Most important he had to have the plans approved by the county. Then he built the floor for the house, which is actually the basement ceiling. He worked alone in wind and snow, moving huge floor joists in place, not an easy task when you're by yourself. I stayed in Sacramento in order to have the house ready for sale. Our plan, once we sell the house, will be to move temporarily anyway into our travel trailer, which is parked right next to the building site. I've also been organizing a "barn raising party" for the Labor Day Weekend. Since it's our Annual Deep Pit Barbecue we

Harriet Bocca

should have plenty of help! Just think Holly, our dreams are coming true, at least the ones we can control.

I'll keep you informed…as we follow our dream!

August 1999

Dear Sweet Holly,

Just a quick note to tell you that I've been thinking about you, as usual. We sold our house in Sacramento and are now up at Summer Lake. We're all ready for our "barn raising party," which will be in a few weeks. Our trailer is just fine for now, but it will be so nice to begin building our little house. I'm looking forward to sitting in my living room this next winter, warmed by the wood burning stove and watching the snow fall. Don has been working night and day to make sure we have all the supplies needed in order to get the job done. Our goal is to get the house sealed and enclosed before winter. As you know winters can be very cold and harsh up at Summer Lake, so we'll need all the protection we can get from the elements. It looks like we're all ready for our "barn raising party," and are we excited! The response from our "flyer" telling of our building plans and the need for help on Labor Day Weekend has been overwhelming. We should have at least 100 people here for about three days to help. It's humbling to have such support, we will never forget their generosity.

Words Spoken Only On Paper

October 1999

Dearest Holly,

Oh, my have we been busy, hardly have time to stop and enjoy.

    Our "barn raising," was a huge success! The weather couldn't have been better and with well over a hundred people arriving days in advance we had more than enough help. Many of them camped on our property and joined us for a community cookout. Others stayed at the local motels or Summer Lake Lodge; some drove hundreds and hundreds of miles. They came, they worked, and they played in the great outdoors. It did our hearts good to have such support and we now have our wonderful little house. One of our friends who is a house painter drove all the way from Los Angeles with his equipment trailer towed behind his motor home. He stayed for about five days and did not leave until the outside of our house was completely painted and protected from the weather. Of course, many of Bert's friends showed up ready to work. They brought their own hammers, work belts, hard hats, and gloves. One motorcycle friend admitted that he knew very little about building a house or even pounding nails but he knew how to get water to the crew and help wherever he could. I saw him working throughout the day picking up nails and sweeping, never stopping. Everyone had fun and I believe they all felt inspired by the simple act of doing and helping out of love. We even had an elderly couple who

Harriet Bocca

really shouldn't have done hard labor so they were our official gofers and picked up construction supplies in town.

While we have so much more to do inside the house, we are grateful that we have had this humbling experience in life, with people who truly care about us. Through the years, our collective friends and family have made friends with each other. Staying connected at our Annual Barbecue, many get together at other times of the year, finding common interests. We will never forget their act of kindness and each and every one should feel that our little house is their little house. However, as I have tried to tell everyone, please call so I can clean the bathroom!

I'd better get going, Don needs a helping hand. We still have sheets and blankets separating our rooms and drywall to hang. Got a little makeshift kitchen with plywood counters, but as Don always says, "trust me," I'll have a beautiful kitchen someday. What I'm looking forward to is an early Christmas present of a real toilet that actually flushes! No more "honey bucket" for me. Can it get any better?

Keep happy dear Holly, stay warm, and know that I will be thinking of you as winter settles in and keeps you from your outdoor garden work. Hugs to your family

Love, me

March 2000

Dear Harriet,

I've been so excited hearing about your prairie house. HOORAY for following your dream! It's a dream that comes from love and was built on and with love, that is beautiful. I love what you were saying about living with the earth again. It's almost always quiet enough to listen to your heart. (PS you have a good heart.) You know when you bought that land; it was the first time my family went to the lake for the summer. I have such good memories of time spent there.

Now that we live in Idaho, I realize that I needed to relocate away from so much of the sad memories of the mountain and all Bert's friends. I still dream about him sometimes, and it is always on the mountain, where we lived for so many years not far from each other, but hardly knowing each other, until we went to high school. He stays just the same but I am always me, now. I miss him when I wake up. I really look forward to seeing him again. Life seems to zoom right by and stand still all at one time. When I look in the mirror I see little wrinkles by my eyes and laugh lines, but I feel sometimes unchanged on the inside. I feel so connected with him, even now. I believe I have and always will know him, and that he watches over my life as a silent friend.

Then there's you. I see and hear so much of him in you. He was a truly good human being. That comes from you, Don and your family. I love knowing you. When I am all alone in nature, looking out over the most beautiful land God made, I think of you and him and say thank you to God. I am continually in awe of what I have been given. I wish you and Don so much love in your BIG adventure. Save a space for me.

Love always, Holly

P.S. Next letter will be lighter I hope.

Words Spoken Only On Paper

April 2000

Dear Holly,

We just returned home from working in Yuma, Arizona and received your sensitive letter; what a perfect day! You are such a pure person who speaks through your heart. I know that's why Bert loved you and respected you. I was especially touched by the way you expressed your sense of present and past, how you realize that your body is growing older, but your heart and soul have stayed true to your spirit. You are still that beautiful person you have always been.

The pictures in my mind of both Bert and his brother Brandon are that they are together and helping each other. I'm not sure if I ever told you, but there is also a third person in my mind's eye. He's my brother Mark, who committed suicide in 1971; he was only thirty-three- years- old. Bert never knew him here on earth, but I know they are with each other now. Mark was such an important part of my life, always there for our kids and me. Bert was conceived three days before Mark died. He was the kind of big brother everyone would want. His frequent visits to our house were the highlight of the week.

Since he was in the medical field, he often worked weekends, and would show up on our doorstep in the middle of the week. This is when our first three children were still small and not in school yet. Don would go off to work, and Mark would help get the kids ready for a day of adventure, often packing a picnic lunch and fishing poles. He was so supportive during the time our daughter was sick with severe asthma, sometimes babysitting so I could have an afternoon off. It was a shock for our whole family when he died. The circumstances of his death were tragic, as he was homosexual and trying to live a socially accepted life. This was at the time when homosexuals were not accepted by society at all! He spent his life taking care of sick and dying people and trying to fit in. Although my Mom and Dad have both died, nothing has been so dramatic in my life as the death of two sons and this special brother. I must admit I cannot bear to think of the pain my two remaining children have suffered and always will, by the death of their brothers and their favorite uncle Mark.

The best thing is that I know that this life is only temporary, we're just passing through, and we'll all be together soon enough. I must believe this! We who are left must do something positive with our loss. I've come to the conclusion that it's not what happens to us, but what we do with what happens. I'm sure I've written about this before and realize that the real loss would have been not to learn and to have been destroyed by self-pity!

You're such an inspiration to me Holly; I can't express how connected I feel to you and your connection with Bert. I know that he's watching over you and he has excellent communication skills. I believe that when we have those moments of overwhelming longing, we are closer to our loved ones as they are visiting with us. Embrace those moments, Holly, and know that you are unique.

Words Spoken Only On Paper

By the way, I understand how you feel about the mountains. There are so many memories of another life on that mountain. It was there that we lived for over eighteen years, raised our children, and became a part of a community. When I visit those memories, I experience how much I not only had, but how much I have lost. This painful process of reality has also given me, as well as you, the ability to evolve. These flashbacks are always emotional yet something I cannot forget, for they are part of me. Just as you dear Holly, our past life experiences are who we are. Now is another time and I've learned to visit those memories in my mind, but try not to stay too long, as the pain is unbearable. However, I would never want to forget them. It's possible to visit there without pain, much like you can re-visit the birth of your child, (the love is all consuming and the physical pain insignificant), but it's an emotional journey.

You've bloomed into a beautiful flower Holly. Through your life experiences, you have matured and become even more beautiful than the young bud you once were. You've struggled through some hard winters and yet you still survive. Without your life experiences you may not have become quite so beautiful.

I started out saying this was the "Perfect Day" because when I write to you, I'm visiting with you on an intimate level and that's perfect. So many people miss such a deep level of expression. You give yourself to me when you write and I hope someday you'll be able to share that with others. It's so extraordinary how you let me in your heart, this takes great courage.

Harriet Bocca

April 18, 2000

    Looks like I'm finally going to finish this letter. I received a call last night regarding an article, which I submitted and will be published next month. It's called, "You'd Better Hurry" and was inspired by a hospice patient of mine. She knew about our plan to follow our dream and build our little house in such a rural area of Nevada. Her advice to me was, "you'd better hurry," so I took that advice and ran with it, after all who would know more than a hospice patient how important each moment is in our lives.

    Take care of yourself and your family, and keep following your dream, as it is who you are. Remember that sometimes we have to change our dreams or make adjustments, but the intentions remain the same. I love you, and will always have a place for you in my heart and next to me on the front porch, watching the eagles soar! Please come anytime.

Love, Harriet

Words Spoken Only On Paper

Watching Eagles Soar

Harriet Bocca

The following article appeared in the Spring 2000 issue of ***Sharing Times – A Newsletter for our Hospice Friends and Community***.

"You'd Better Hurry"

An Inspiring Story by Harriet Bocca

An experience in life and death, shared by a hospice Volunteer and her patient, two souls helping each other.

I was led into the living room where a fragile woman with a porcelain-like complexion was sitting. Her smile was contagious as she, with great effort, lifted her head and extended her hand in friendship.

I had been assigned by Hospice to provide companionship and support, not only to her, but also to her caregiver. My volunteer position was part of the interdisciplinary team of professionals who became such an important component to her comfort and care. The cancer had taken its toll on her body and she was dying, but her spirit was intact.

As the weeks went by our visits were filled with valuable moments of sharing private thoughts and nurturing companionship. Our friendship soon became one of trust as she confided to me some of her fears and doubts about life and death. She often reminisced about her earlier years as wife and mother and the kind of life she had lived. Her silent tears when she mentioned the death of her husband and the longing she had to be with him were intimate and profound. Their marriage of over fifty years had been filled with love and special bonding. She beamed with pride as she spoke of her children and grandchildren and then her eyes filled with tears. Her life was coming to an end. At each visit, I witnessed a fading of the stamina she needed to hold her head up or speak loud enough to converse. Her strength was ebbing as she struggled to finish a sentence or complete a thought. Her need to have someone with her was strong and she would slip in and out of awareness as I read passages from her favorite book, the Bible.

Just before she died, she gave me a most remarkable gift, the gift of wisdom. I had shared with her a dream my husband and I had for well over twenty years. Our dream was to build a "little house on the prairie" far away from the big city life.

This dream had been a source of great solace and hope for us. As I shared my dreams and fears, she listened intently. Then she seemed to gain new energy and suddenly her eyes grew bright and she reached out her hands and squeezed mine tightly. Looking straight at me and with the wisdom of a woman who knew about life and death, she simply said, "You'd better hurry." These wise words became my seed of hope and gave me courage. Soon afterwards, my husband and I began to take action and make our dream a reality. Through her words, she reminded me of what I had already known, but let slip away: Life is precious and each moment given is an opportunity not to be missed, for our moments combined are the sum of our life.

The gift of the three little words, "You'd better hurry," which were spoken in the late afternoon of this special woman's life, was indeed revealing. Someday when I too have to face my afternoon of life, I know I will have used my precious moments wisely.

July 2000

Dear Holly,

What a busy summer we've had. I hope yours has been busy and fun as well. Seems like we just get home from traveling/working, spend a few day's unpacking and watering, then we're off to Home Depot to get some more supplies to work on our house. We now have doors for all the rooms, but love to keep them open as it makes everything brighter and helps cool us off by the predictable afternoon breeze. Sometimes it's more like a windstorm, that's when we hunker down and watch a good movie or read. By the way, our windmill really gets going good on windy afternoons and our photovoltaic system is working out great since we get so much sun. We live just like most people, switching on a light or watching TV when we like. However, we have learned to respect the use of power, and monitor our use carefully. It's a good lesson for our grandchildren as well.

Today we borrowed our brother-in-law's old tractor and worked on clearing up some of the land we had disrupted last winter when we put in our septic tank. I hadn't realized how much work developing the land and building a house would be, however it's been well worth it. I know I'm getting older and don't have the energy I use to have. Each morning I start great, helping Don carry drywall, planting trees, moving rocks, yet come lunch time I want to stop, eat and take a nap! I can't imagine why!

Our weather has been hot and our little house needs a front porch desperately. The afternoon sun can be brutal and our trees are not big enough to provide shade. A good friend has offered to drive down from Washington the week before our Annual Barbecue and help work on our porch. We've been using a makeshift step just to get in the house, so imagine how wonderful it will be to have a real porch with real steps and a covered front porch. Just think, it will be one-step closer to a life of leisure! I wonder if that will ever happen.

Enclosed you'll find a little gift. I saw these angel cards and knew that they were for you. They're something to hold in your hand, touch gently and send to loved ones. I have met many wonderful people in my life, who have done incredibly kind acts of love, but I've only met two full time real angels! I recognize the difference, because an angel does good naturally, when no one is looking. I believe that Steve's mom, Christine, is a true angel, as she has shown constant goodness through all these years, in small and quiet ways. The other angel is you! You were chosen to be the one I could turn to for safety and protection and helped buffer my fall with your wings. Through your letters of love, you give me a safe place to express my fears, without judgment. Now that I have thought about it, I realize that I have a number of truly good people in my life who are like angels to me. Their kind acts and true benevolence including courage has made my heart a little lighter.

Like you, I have wonderful moments of memories, yet the shadow of loss is always hovering, casting darkness over my heart. I've learned to live without, but I'm not happy about it! Please forgive me for sounding like I'm being dragged and screaming thought life. Sometimes when I self-indulge in pity, I feel just like that. However, somewhere, deep within, I know I want to see this to the end; I have too many things to do…places to go…people to see!

Take care of yourself, give a hug to your family, and keep your wings up!

Love, Harriet

August 2000

Dear Harriet,

    I have indeed had a busy and fun summer. I sat down to write a list for something, (I'm a list person), and just started thinking of you. I re-read the last letter you wrote me and as always, I was smiling. Tears and smiles are always hand in hand with you. Such is life! Anyway, back to the letter, I'm reading this letter and thinking, that's not me, that's you! Your heart humbles me; you have supported me though my life in a way that is so amazing. I feel safe to open my most inside place and know that there is no judgment or even disappointment. Unfortunately, in the inside are also the things that break our hearts and in those self-pity meltdowns you are there too. Even if, it must be, it is painful because my pains are also your pains. Never in my lifetime could I ever explain what you mean

Harriet Bocca

Holly"s Garden

to me, not even to myself. I know you are a gift. OK enough said, thank you.

Life continues to amaze me! Nicolet just started the third grade. What a remarkable age. She is so much herself, it's lovely.

We're looking for property or a house here in Idaho and quite nervous about the decision. We're really hesitant though, as it's a pretty grown-up thing to do. It's so exciting; I plan on having a huge garden filled with flowers and vegetables. I'll spend my mornings working in the soil, harvesting my crop and afternoons writing. It will be so much fun to be able to tell you about my house in the woods of Idaho. I truly love this place, it's part of my soul. Since we have so many rivers and streams close by, I have become quite the fly fisherwoman. We had an amazing fishing and camping summer, even traveled as far up north as Jasper National Park in Canada. It was so beautiful in Jasper and a great little town with friendly people. I have a good Grizzly bear experience to tell you about, but I will save it for a "porch story"

Harriet Bocca

I hope to see you face to face; perhaps I can "will" it to be. It would be nice to make it to your barbecue "shindig," a word I learned from Bert.

Love, Holly

September 2000

Dear Holly,

I've been waiting to get a few quiet moments to spend some time with you, so here I am!

Your last letter was so sensitive and beautiful, just like you! I recognize that you have grown into a beautiful woman, yet it always amazes me to feel your strength through your writing. Even though we are both growing older, I will always see you as a young girl, as you seem frozen in time.

The pocket angels you sent recently are so sweet and very special. I will use mine to hang onto when things get tough and frightening. Since it's a gift from you, I know it's powerful.

Our barbecue turned out great! Lots of good friends and family arrived staying for days. As you know, many drive up in their RV and set up camp; some stay at nearby motels and all have a great time.

Words Spoken Only On Paper

I must admit that it's gotten a lot bigger and more work than we had ever imagined. Most of those who join us have been there for us through some tough times, they have held us up when we almost fell. Their sustaining support has kept us going, that and a lot of hard work. Heck, most of them helped build our house!

By the way, our house is coming along great; we gathered huge stones from around our property and built a firewall and hearth for our wood burning fireplace. Don had never done anything like that before but it turned out beautiful, a bit stressful but it's still in place. The solar panels are capturing enough energy for us to run most things we need. We've learned to respect the use of power and monitor our use carefully, in other words you won't see us leaving the lights on when we don't need them.

Next week we'll be on our way to San Diego, we'll travel down the coast of California, which is a gorgeous drive. It's the same route we took the day Bert died. I remember what a beautiful peaceful day it was; our stops along the coast, picnicking on the sand and watching the seagulls soar high in the sky searching for their lunch in the water below. Looking back it seems it was a moment frozen in time, something to vision in preparation for the night ahead. Life can change in an instant, how well we know.

My love and appreciation to you Holly, you help give me a place to be me.

Love, Harriet

Harriet Bocca

March 2001

Dear Holly,

After what seemed like a long cold winter, we're finally enjoying a bit of spring. All the trees are budding and the weeds are shooting up from the ground pushing small rocks out of the way, as if to celebrate the coming of something great. Each morning a small group of deer shows up at our front door looking for breakfast. It's a wonder they don't knock and want coffee. But I guess it's the fresh green clumps of grass which have sprouted up all around our house that are attractive to them. We watch them out our kitchen window, as it's such a nice vantage point sipping our morning coffee and greeting our new day. Witnessing these wild creatures, in their natural habitat, reminds me of what they must feel like captured in a zoo. They look so free and undisturbed in my front yard. When I see one interested in my young pine trees, I do feel very protective for my tree. That's when I run outside like a half crazy person yelling at "Bambi" and friends to stay away from my tree! I'm much like Captain Morton, played by James Cagney in the movie *Mr. Roberts*. The movie takes place on a U.S. Navy ship sometime during WWII. Captain Morton is obsessed with his prize possession, which is a somewhat pathetic looking palm tree, planted in a huge pot, and located on the deck outside his quarters. He keeps an eye on that tree day and night, it seems that's the only thing he keeps an eye on, forgetting all others and the needs of his men. He will go to any length to make sure the tree is protected. Obviously, he goes nuts if anybody even gets near the tree! Well, that's kind of like me if a cute little deer gets near one of my pine trees. I go a little nuts, but I get over it with a second cup of coffee.

Last week we were down in the Los Angeles area on business. While there we got a chance to visit with our son Laurence and his family. We had to make a decision about Bert's dog, whose name was Digger. We knew it was time to say goodbye to him, as his quality of life had really gone downhill. He no longer could control his bladder and his eyesight was bad. His old body had just worn out, so we had him put to sleep on March 12. It was hard to do but we know he had a good life with lots of love and attention; perhaps he is now keeping Bert company, as he was his "best friend" for such a long time.

Due to our traveling, we didn't know what to do with Digger right after Bert died. Christine and her son Steve offered to take him. I believe Christine is one of the kindest, purest people I know. They were so devastated by Bert's death, I think they needed something of his to help get through the hard times. They loved Bert and thought of him as part of their family as so many others. After a number of years, Laurence moved to a place off the mountain, with a fenced in backyard, so he was able to care for Digger. Unfortunately, I never felt that Digger was where he was supposed to be; after all, he was a mountain dog!

Harriet Bocca

Bert's Dog Digger

Digger was the second dog in our life…, Brandon picked out our first dog, Jiggs, just before Bert was born. Jiggs had light colored long hair and was just about the same size as Digger. I remember how protective he was when I brought Bert home from the hospital. He would sit on the floor, right next to the chair I sat in as I nursed Bert. If anyone would even approach the house he would growl and if it was a man, he'd bark! His barking never seemed to stop after that, guess that was when he became our protector. He never did this before Bert was born. It was as if he knew I needed to be taken care of in a special way, as I was responsible for such a special new life. When Bert was able to scoot around, Jiggs would often lay right next to his blanket and protect him. He never got on the blanket, but very close. Both dogs were very similar and great family pets. We had Digger for twelve years. It's strange how Bert and Brandon died before their dogs, guess the dogs figured they were still needed. They were good loving animals and brought a lot of joy to our family. As Bert said on the day he brought Digger home, "I'm just a little boy Mom, I need a dog!" Maybe Digger needed Bert.

Our travel schedule is getting hectic, but we always see and learn new things. It's a big world out there Holly, go out and enjoy it with your family. Remember if you are ever in our area, please stop by, our bed and breakfast is usually open and we even serve dinner!

I love you, Harriet

Harriet Bocca

June 2002

Dear Harriet,

    I hope this letter finds you with a smile on your face. Our family is good all healthy, happy and glad for summer to come! Since it's warm here for such a short time, everyone celebrates when the sun comes out and the temperature goes over 70 degrees! So summer is like one long party until September when the nights turn colder and thoughts of winter creep into our minds.

    BIG NEWS! I'm going to have a baby, a baby boy! I am due in September and very excited. Nothing beats the happiness that Nicolet radiates over the baby. She loves this baby unconditionally before she even has gotten a chance to see him. It's so much fun to wait for him with her. This pregnancy has been so amazing in changing me. I think it has helped heal the girl I was the first time around. To be healthy in spirit and you're own self makes it different. Today is my eighth anniversary and it is easy to look back over those years. Tony, Nicolet and I have grown up together and I think we are very close because of that. At ten-years-old our daughter grows more like a little lady every day and is absolutely beautiful. Her personality is so easy going and she has such a sentimental way about her. This girl is all life! Tony and I both agree that she is the greatest thing we will have ever done with this lifetime.

    I still think of Bert during my life's most important events. It is easier now to celebrate them with him, for him, I know that is what he would want now. I like to think that my life is better because I knew him and he loved me. I am trying not to look for so many answers anymore and just soaking it all up instead. Who knows how long I have here either? Thank you for letting me tell you my secrets over these years, Harriet.

Me

Harriet Bocca

June 2002

Dear Holly,

Perhaps we were best buds in another life, perhaps you and Bert were? Each time I read your beautiful letter a tear comes to my eyes. I haven't been able to really cry for years, guess it's my way to stay in control.

Your news of having a baby boy is so terrific! You sound so content and happy. I know Nicolet will be such a good big sister. Tony has obviously grown with you and now together you will welcome another child and what a lucky kid he'll be.

How are your house plans? Are you still able to plan on building? I know it's a big step but keep holding onto your dream. We're still working on our house and I must admit at times it's very frustrating. I hadn't realized all the work that it would take once the outside was done. Since Don has been busy these last six months, things are going very slow. We need the income but I sure would like to have a kitchen with real counters, not plywood, and a decent floor would be life changing.

It's good that you and Tony started dreaming your dream at such an early age, it gives you more time to get it done. Don and I are almost 59-years-old, guess we'd better hurry.

Today we're in central California working. It's beautiful, so nice and green. Since this is a large fruit and vegetable farming area there are plenty of roadside stands selling the best of the summer harvest. Last night we had fresh corn on the cob cooked in the microwave and a big green salad. We learned from a friend how to cook corn in the microwave, but if it's really fresh I like to eat it raw! Next week we'll be in Gilroy, California and spend some time at the Garlic Festival. I hear they have garlic ice cream! You know we'll have to try that.

According to neighbors in Summer Lake we have two major forest fires in the area. Our home is safe so far but most of our neighbors up the canyon have been evacuated. Events like fires, floods, and natural disasters of any kind seem to bring people together. I wish I could be there to help. I've let it be known that our house is available if need be.

Please keep us informed of your upcoming special event, we are so excited for you. Have a wonderful lazy summer and keep healthy.

Love Harriet

September 2002

Harriet,

Today is my due date, and I think I'm in pre-labor, but not sure! Got the first snow

Harriet Bocca

dusting in the mountains behind my house, so I think today is a good day for a baby.

I hope you and Don are happy and healthy out on the homestead. We're trying for April to start our house. Tony's back surgery and my pregnancy put this year's plans on hold. If all goes well, we will be in our new house by the baby's first birthday. I have thought of you and Bert throughout my pregnancy, as I always do when any significant life event takes place, and I always give a little thanks to you.

Love, Holly

We received an announcement that Holly had her baby boy on October 1st, Bert's birth day, they named him Sammy, and mother and baby are doing great!

November 2002

Dear Holly,

How exciting to hear that Sammy has arrived all safe and cuddly. I can just picture you snuggled up with him in your safe little home where there is only love. I'll bet at times it seems that your heart is going to burst!

A little boy will be such fun and quite different from a girl. It will be an adventure just getting to know each other. I'm sure he already has a great personality especially with a big sister around to stimulate him and his imagination. Nicolet will become his best friend as they teach each other new stuff, and I'll bet Tony has a tool belt all ready for Sammy to help him build your new house.

How I envy those quiet moments you'll spend with this little one, Holly. Although 3 a.m. feedings are rough, they don't last long. There's something so wonderful about the intimate act of bonding in the middle of the night, when no one else is around. How lucky Sammy is to have such a loving family to welcome him into this world.

Of course, I am overwhelmed that Sammy was born on Bert's birth day! As I read your announcement aloud to Don and got to the date of birth, I couldn't continue. I finally pulled myself together and finished the announcement. Both Don and I hugged each other and shared our feelings about such a significant event. Some may think we are overreacting, but it's such a profound coincidence, or is it?

I'll keep in touch and be thinking about all of you.

Love, Harriet

Harriet Bocca

June 2003

Dear Harriet,

    You enter my thoughts so frequently, but this beautiful little seven-month-old keeps me turning circles these days! Happy Mother's Day to you Harriet Bocca.

    I forgot how much work babies are and I don't remember being so tired last time. I think I was a little perkier eleven years ago. With that aside, I am utterly in love with Sammy! He is everything good and beautiful in life all rolled up in one fat baby! At 21 pounds, he's a bundle of joy! It has been so much fun to have another baby at such a different time in my life and then to have my lovely Nicolet right by my side. She is so amazing and funny and smart, she makes me feel so confident as Sammy's mommy. They are my greatest accomplishments. It's neat to watch Tony with his baby boy! Mostly I love the way Sammy loves his mommy. The way we know each other is magic, like he has been mine for all of time. I like to think some special people in heaven have protected him over the last ten years. I love that he was born two weeks late so he could share my Grandma Eva's and Bert's birthday, two special people in my life. I thought of you too that day and the never-ending circle of love we have for our children. I think it is what unconditional love is all about and can last through all of time.

    I hope this hasn't made you sad in any way, I believe it is just another way we are connected to each other.

I cherish you,

Love, Holly

August 2003

Dear Holly,

    It's about time I get this down on paper as it's what is inside of me. As you know, it's close to the anniversary of Bert's death. I've always attempted to keep busy during the times of the year when events occurred that caused unbearable pain. Both Brandon and Bert's death dates are obviously painful, yet I've learned to cope. I'm not so good at it sometimes, but I haven't figured out what else to do.

Harriet Bocca

Since Don is out of town this week and the anniversary date is coming up I've made plans to go to a gigantic rummage sale. This will be fun since I've invited a friend who needs to keep busy and have fun too! Her husband died last year and her grandson has recently been diagnosed with a serious illness. Our rummage sale outing will keep our minds busy instead of thinking about our problems. We cannot change these things.

However, my internal voice keeps pulling me to other thoughts. I wonder how different my life would be if our boys were alive. I know that Laurence and Anne lost part of their childhood memories, which was a big part of who they were, when their brothers died. No matter what I do I can't make the hurt go away. It's unbearable at times to witness Don struggle with his feelings. He holds everything inside, yet suffers just the same. I know he's having his own "pity party" and I'm not invited.

We're grateful that Bert's friends have gone on with their lives. They needed to and neither Don nor I would have wanted them to be stuck in sorrow. We love to share in their lives and help celebrate their successes, knowing they are OK makes us OK.

You, my dear, have been the most remarkable friend of all! I guess women tend to be nurtures by nature and you definitely have done that and more, not only to Bert but also to me. Perhaps that's why you are such a remarkable mother. Your notes and letters through the years have been a confirmation of love for your children and your husband. I feel privileged to have you in my life and know I always will. Perhaps one day you'll be able to write a book about your life, as you have such a wonderful way of expressing yourself, strong yet vulnerable.

We both have learned life goes on, and it can be filled with wonderful moments, which we wouldn't have wanted to miss. A few years ago while reading a self-help book I came across a question, which was fascinating to me. I began asking people the question which the book inspired and was amazed at some of their answers. Here's the question; "If you could be anyone in the whole world living or dead, who would you want to be?" My answer was fast and with no doubt, I would want to be myself. Others have to think about it, which is not the intent, since we usually edit our answer when we think. Since there is no right or wrong answer, it doesn't matter what you answer, it's more of a thought provoking question. It is quite amazing given the sorrow of the death of two children that I would answer that way but I know that I want to live this life given to me. I need to see what I can do with my time, and if I can make a difference. I believe our life is the one true thing that we own and we are responsible for our actions or lack of actions.

My afternoon plans for today will be to continue watering since we have about forty trees now, and watering is a big job. Of course, our trees are nothing like the pine and evergreens that you're surrounded by, but there're wonderful given the harsh environment we have out here in the sticks. I have so much fun driving around our place tending to them in my old golf cart, which I call Maynard. Oftentimes I park in the shade of a tree and soak up the view, I just can't get enough.

Harriet Bocca

Sometimes around noon, before it gets too hot, I'll stop and take a break. This is when you can find me on my front porch gazing across the valley. My view is of the lake off to the right, green pastures and of course the gigantic mountains! Since we recently planted a little grass and put up a white picket fence, (everyone needs a white picket fence in the front yard), I'm peaceful in my paradise. It's also fun to watch the bunnies romp around in their new playground of green grass in the desert. By the way, before I sit in my comfortable rocker, I always check to make sure there are no snakes! We had a rattlesnake take a morning nap under the porch a while back and refused to leave. I was just fine not knowing he was there, but when he rattled, it was so loud and hard to ignore! It's interesting how a rattlesnake will stand its ground, this one just wanted not to be disturbed. This evening I'll take Maynard, my brightly colored pink golf cart, and drive across the road and up on the little hill, which overlooks the whole valley. There, I'll watch the sunset and talk to myself and perhaps God will be listening.

So my dear, I will say goodbye for now, I know it's your birthday time, so I'm sending a little check. I hope you can get something for yourself or surprise the family with something special. An ice cream party sounds fun! One of these days I'm going to get up there and meet your newest addition as well as see Nicolet, I'll bet she's really grown up!

Happy Birthday to you, enjoy your life!

Love, Harriet

Words Spoken Only On Paper

February 2004

Dear Harriet,

    Thank you for the Christmas gift and your yearly newsletter. I always like to hear about your adventures out on the range. It sounds like the secrets out, though, with all your new neighbors moving in. It has grown a lot here too. Quite a few of my family have moved here as well as a good friend of ours.

    Nicolet turned 12 in January and there is no stopping Sammy. He's 16-months-old and it takes all of us to keep up with him. He's the absolute apple of my eye. I am enjoying my role as mommy very much and have learned enough to know how quickly it will go by. I can hardly believe my baby girl is twelve already and I'm thirty! It's been twelve years since I've seen your beautiful son. I must tell you he has been on my mind a lot lately. I used to think that surely time would put those old feelings away somewhere, but am always surprised at how fresh they really are. I try not to question what if, but find myself doing just that. I dreamed about him on the full moon in January. These dreams are few and far between and leave me feeling desperate afterwards, desperate to talk to him. So I get out my "Bert box" when I have a moment to myself (usually very late at night) and I look at 1 of 2 pictures I have of him. I like that I am a girl and I remember what an amazing boy, person he was. Honestly, knowing and losing him is the single most life-altering thing that has ever happened to me and the birth of my children is the other, especially Nicolet. It is funny to me that they really happened almost at the same time. A birth and a death, to find out I have a soul, a spirit! What a bittersweet gift. I miss him now too, as an adult. I miss having him part of my life. Therefore, I guess I was wrong in thinking time would put it behind me because I have found that I will just have to wait to see him again. Time only gives me more stories to tell him. I have a feeling he's been watching it all take place and maybe he'll have stories for me instead.

As I am getting to the end of my letter, I am questioning if I should mail this or not? I don't want to make you hurt too. If you're reading this, I guess you know what I decided. Please know how much I cherish my friendship with you and how grateful I truly am for letting me empty my heart to you all of these years.

Love, Holly

March 2004

Dear sweet Holly,

What an incredible letter you wrote. Never, ever be afraid to let me in your heart! If I cry, I cry. Crying can be a good thing. Those feelings of Bert are always with me and like you, I just find a safe place to put them so people don't think I'm totally nuts!

    It has always put my heart at ease to know that Bert has had you to nurture and love him in life and in death. I do worry about you holding on to him so tight, but your letters reveal that you recognized that life continues to grow, just as you have grown. You, my, dear have filled your life with love, how could you do anything different? I would

Harriet Bocca

never want his memory and your relationship with him to interfere with your marriage and ability to be a whole person, and neither would he.

I believe you and I are on the same page with our grief. We both had to go on with our lives because there is so much loving and living to do. Neither you nor I could simply crawl into a hole and stop. What would be the point? Therefore, we go forward, sometimes struggling to find an easier path to take, sometimes falling backwards, yet we continue. Oftentimes when I find myself extremely happy, I feel guilty. How can I reach such happiness when I carry around this huge hole in my heart? I guess that's why it's called the grief process, as we continue to go through many emotions and up's and downs, while trying to fix our hearts.

We've been busy haven't we? You have evolved into an extraordinary loving wife and mother. Please, please write in a journal as often as you can, for you have so much insight and are so giving in your writings. Tell about your everyday life and the big beautiful world of Idaho. Write about the snow as it falls outside your kitchen window, write where your mind wanders when doing dishes. Let the world know how your heart feels when you see a wounded bird fall from its nest or your baby crawling on the floor. You have such talent Holly I know you should share your life with others; they need your insight. People need to know that life can be good, even if tough things happen. They need to realize that all they have to do is find peace in the simple little things around them. They need to get in touch with themselves, to hear their heart beat and be still and quiet enough to listen. You've found this peace in your life and you can help others find peace too.

I've managed to live more than sixty years and am just finding out how to appreciate all the wonderful small things. To stop and look at life differently, without pre-conceived ideas, allows me to find out something new about myself every day. I must admit that I'm not always pleased with what I see, as I should have learned more. It's then I realize that I have lived my life for a purpose and the learning process is never ending. I know that writing is my real purpose. My life experiences have given me the insight to help others and myself. Just like you, I write with my heart.

Since my life is filled with extremes, I'm either busy traveling or home alone while Don's traveling I have found I plan my days at my own pace. It's quite interesting, much like living in limbo as I drift from day to day. Something fun must always be on my list of things to do, perhaps work outside, or read a good book. Exercise is another activity that's on the list, as I know I need to keep moving. However, I'm not always successful at this and can find all kinds of excuses. It's either too hot, too cold, too windy or I'm too tired! Nevertheless, I do try! Since we live almost an hour from civilization (city dweller's opinion), friends and family often ask if I get lonely all by myself. I can honestly say that it's lonely at times, but it's wonderful to be by myself...I'm comfortable with me!

This weekend I'll be traveling with my sister to visit relatives. Thank you again for the beautiful letter. Don and I shared tears together when I read it aloud. You inspire me in so many ways.

Harriet Bocca

Hope to see you and your family soon, I'll bet Sammy is adorable. It lightens my heart to know that you have so many people around you who care about you and can be supportive in your life.

I will always love you,   Harriet

April 2004

Dear Harriet and Don too,

Thank you so much for your unconditional friendship! I am sorry for being so down and sending you that letter. The long winter doesn't help even though I love snow and long evenings of uninterrupted family time. Perhaps I just have too much time to think.

Today the sun is out and spring has begun to sprung! Sammy and I have been playing outside every day and there is finally no snow left in my yard. For an eighteen-month-old boy, after a very long winter, this new freedom is the best. Since he is now walking he has so much to explore outside. He loves to just walk and walk out in the woods. Lucky for me he seems to like being in our garden and since that is my favorite place we are "two peas in a pod." It's pretty big and deer proof, so Sammy can just run wild in there. I can't plant anything for another few months but there's a lot of work already.

Our business is starting to pick up as people need repairs and remodels. I know summer will be here before I blink an eye. I'm excited to start working in the garden and plan on planting raspberries as they are delicious. Everything from the garden is delicious! Nicolet, who just informed me she has only two months of school left, is now old enough to help me make preserves with all those great berries.

I hope I didn't worry you with my last letter. Sometimes I miss Bert so much in the physical, and then I realize he's right here with all of us and watching over my family. I feel protected. Tony and I often have talks about this and he's always impressed with how many beautiful things came from your son. While he didn't know him very well, he has come to know him through our friendship.

Hope you're all well!

Harriet Bocca

Love, Holly

July 2004

Dear Holly,

As the anniversary of Bert's death speeds closer on the calendar, I'm drawn to thoughts of you. The flashbacks of his death and that time in my life occur many times throughout the year, but the hot summer months are especially difficult.

It's hard to believe that so many years have passed yet the smallest of details are still just a blink away. I remember you standing behind me at the mortuary, and the beautiful white roses you gifted to me, a remembrance of Bert. I felt so bad that you had to wait so long. It seems that the whole town had come to support all of us and the lines of people went on forever. However, of all his friends and family you have been the one who has kept his memory alive through your thoughtfulness and love.

As a family we talk of Bert and Brandon, sometimes laugh at the funny things they said or did. However, we can't get too deep into our yearning and loss as we all get depressed and withdraw from the conversation. I guess we go into our own little hole and can't dig out, as it's far too painful.

Butterflies Fluttering

Harriet Bocca

Tomorrow Don and I are on our way to Gold Beach on the coast of Oregon. We're looking forward to cooling off since the weather here has been hot and windy. My little patch of grass is looking somewhat sad but the rose bushes are doing great! It seems so odd to come across our place out here in the sticks, people don't expect our little oasis in such an arid, isolated place. Our house is almost complete, although I'm not sure if a house you build yourself is ever fully completed. It's a far cry from when we first started living out here in our travel trailer and then moving into our unfinished house with sheets and blankets separating the rooms. I remember so well that first winter, and the best Christmas gift ever, a toilet that actually flushed! Wow, we've come a long way!

You'll have to come see what I've done to my guest room. A beautiful greeting card you sent me in April inspired me. It was covered with butterfly's fluttering into a shaft of sunlight in the woods with light filtering through the trees. The peacefulness of the card stirred something creative in me, so I designed a mural, which loosely reproduced the scene. The room is painted cotton candy pink; I call it my garden room since it reminds me of my fantasy garden. I even painted a tree in the corner with the help of a few family members. Believe me it took courage to paint that tree, but now the room is absolutely my favorite room in the house! I'm not sure how my guests like it, but since we don't charge for lodging they seem to adjust. I even leave sunglasses on the desk in case it's too bright for them.

Are you still planning to build your house? I know you've had to put your plans on hold, but I hope you never lose sight of your dream. Perhaps I should say, never be afraid to dream! I found a saying in a magazine recently, which I love to repeat. "There are people who "shoulda, woulda, coulda", and there are people who are glad they did!" I know that you and Tony are glad that you moved to such a beautiful place, have amazing children and love each other deeply. You have chosen a lifestyle, which focuses on the real foundations of happiness. You have made time to appreciate the small and simple things, which make life worth living. I'm so glad Bert brought you into my life.

Love, Harriet

We received another beautiful handmade Christmas card from Holly along with a short note.

December 2005

Dear Harriet and Don,

I hope this reaches you with smiles on your faces. We will be in your area for the month of February and wanted to know if you will be home. I would love to see you and for you to finally meet Sammy. Nicolet will be fourteen in January and Sammy turned three on his last birthday. We put an extra candle on his cake for Bert and one for my Grandma, her birthday too!

Our business is doing good, we even had to hire extra help, so we're keeping busy, and of course we spend a lot of time chasing after Sammy.

You are always in my thoughts and I know that someday we'll be able to sit and chat.

Hope to see you soon. I'm sending love from the wilderness and Blessings for the Holidays.

I love you both - Holly, Tony, Nicolet and Sammy

Words Spoken Only On Paper

December 2005

Dear sweet Holly,

Last month we had an opportunity to travel to Italy for a consulting job. What an amazing experience and one we will never forget. We were assigned an interpreter who was young, tall, and handsome, and of course, helpful. Our assignment was in a small town a few hours from Venice and Verona. Obviously Venice is well known for its history and famous canals and Verona is famous for its century old coliseum and the story of Romeo and Juliet. Both places are steeped in history and romance, however the best part of the trip was getting to know the people and how they live. We would like to go back someday and explore other places as Italy has so much charm and the people have an amazing respect for their culture. It seems like the more we travel the more we want to know.

Have a wonderful Christmas Holly; we will definitely be looking for you in February. How about a get-together with some of Bert's friends and your friends while you're in the area? I'm thinking of a barbecue with the whole gang, it's been years since we've seen some of them and it will be good to reconnect.

Hugs to you all, Harriet

Harriet Bocca

Romantic Venice, Italy

Words Spoken Only On Paper

June 2006

Hello there,

It's finally looking like summer here at Summer Lake. We've been home since early May and it seems like all I've been doing is weeding and watering. Now I'm not complaining as I really love to work in the outdoors, especially when it's so beautiful, but my body complains a lot!

I bet it's really gorgeous up there at this time of the year, I guess that would go for any time of the year if you like snow. Since we lived in snow country for so many years, I pretty much had my fill of that white stuff which included plenty of shoveling and putting on snow chains. I do know that a fresh snowfall is awesome. The one thing we both seem to have in common and love is the peacefulness of our rural areas, no city noises, nor bright lights at night. Heck, the only thing bright at night around here is the stars.

Now that we spend winters in the lower desert of California, we have grown accustomed to the conveniences of city life. The best part is that we are closer to our hometown and friends. Our visit with you and your family was amazing. Sammy and Nicolet are growing up so fast, Sammy is all boy and Nicolet is so sweet and beautiful. Of course, the get together with so many of Bert's friends was emotional. It was good to see that they all have grown up into the men they were destined to become. I've always believed that it takes a good woman to make a boy a man. Most of the boys have good women and those who are still single will just have to learn on their own.

As you may know this last winter, I became a volunteer CASA, which is a Court Appointed Special Advocate for foster children. It's an amazing job, which can help make a difference in a child's life. The requirements to become a CASA involved special training and of course, thorough background checks as well as a live scan. CASA's are similar to a social worker in that we have access to all information that involves our child. We usually have one or two cases at a time compared to a social worker who may have as many as thirty cases. I feel like all those who work with the child are a team, with the primary social worker in charge. However, I know that I have the power to request and receive information that may have been missed or forgotten and can help give the child a voice in court. I believe this job will take passion and tenacity and I was never so proud as the day I was sworn in as an officer of the court. I know I'm not done with making a difference in life and accomplishing meaningful things. I'm simply not done yet!

Tomorrow is Father's Day and Don is in Missouri but will be home on Monday. It's always a tough time for us, as our obvious void is intensified. To hear everyone go around wishing people happy this and happy that is painful. Our sorrow is not their sorrow but my internal voice sometimes wants to scream at them or at God. This self-inflicted pity party doesn't last too long as I know it serves no purpose and I've got things to do with my life.

On to better and bigger, how is your garden growing this year? I know it's a lot of work, but oh so neat to go out each day and see the fruits of your labor, vegetables too! Last winter my little garden did pretty good. We had a good crop of cabbage, lettuce, green onions, chives and cilantro. I'm not sure if I'll get my garden in for this summer, here at the lake. The problem is that we irrigate with water that is pumped into a large tank by our windmill and then gravity flow to our trees. While we can always pump with our generator, we try to use the wind to do our pumping which makes it difficult to water everything when we're not here. The good news is that the lake is full, since we've had so much snow this winter and all the ranchers who rely on snow melt will receive all the water they need to keep their crops growing and cows happy. You know the saying; a happy cow is a contented cow or is it a happy wife?

Harriet Bocca

Happy Cows

Words Spoken Only On Paper

So let's see, is Nicolet now in the ninth grade? Oh, boy I bet Tony is going to watch the boys' real close as they start hanging around, perhaps he'll put them to work. I'm sure Sammy's gotten big enough to really help his daddy, bet he even has a tool belt.

    I hear the wind kicking up so I'd better go make sure our windmill is turned on so we can use the wind to our advantage. Don't you just love it, nature power!

    Take care of yourself and family, I'll be thinking about you and hope you have a great summer.

Love, Harriet

Holly sent a whimsical card of an outhouse in the woods with a momma bear and her cubs on the front, the caption read, "Just sittin' here thinkin' of you", and inside it said, "and thinkin' of you…and thinkin' of you…The card was very appropriate as we actually have an outhouse on our property.

Harriet Bocca

November 2006

Hello Harriet & Don,

   I like this card and knew I had to get it for you, because I am always "thinkin' and thinkin'" of you! It's November here in the high country, so it is cold and cloudy and will be for the next five months. I turned thirty-three in August and couldn't help but think of my eighteenth birthday which was only a few days after losing my friend Bert. I was also four months pregnant. Since that time, I have recognized that pivotal moment, for me and truly the beginning of a new road in life. His death and the birth to come, made me look at me and helped me decide who I wanted to be. I hate always-bringing Bert up when I write, but with fifteen years having passed, I really wanted to tell you how much he lives on. You know this already because he was important to so many people! I believe he would be proud of who I became, perhaps the person he saw in me before. I have felt obligated to be a good friend. To always, believe in magic and love, never give up, and remember to count my blessings.

In other words, always live! It has been my honor to have been inspired by the friendship he gave me. I feel so thankful and hope I have honored his life, by living mine. Enough said!

Sammy is now four, and Nicolet who is fifteen, is in the ninth grade. She likes high school and as most teenagers, argues a lot with her mother. I know I am protective, yet she is also like an old friend to me. A few weeks ago, she and I went to the big city to see a Brooks and Dunn concert. We had so much fun, she's my best companion for "chick flicks", shopping and hanging out. She's growing so fast and it's scary knowing I'll have to let her go, but I know I will have to so she can live her life. I pray a lot!

We plan to visit family in California for Christmas and I'm going to the Bahamas for New Years with my sisters! I have never been anywhere tropical so I'm pretty excited.

I send you love in this envelope,

Holly

Harriet Bocca

February 2008

Dear Harriet and Don,

   Timing is everything when it comes to me putting my thoughts for you on paper. I never feel like I fully express all of the things I want to say.

   It's been a long winter, seems like I just couldn't get going, but now I feel like my mojo is up and running once again.

   In early January, Tony went to visit family down south where it's brighter and much warmer in the winter. Since Sammy's not in school yet, it was a good opportunity for the two to get away together. Nicolet and I stayed home, since she needed to stay in school. With both gone it made for a very quiet household, which was great for about a week, but then it really hit me. I tend to be a very private person, yet all this alone time without my five- year old and husband, was very unfamiliar territory. I felt a little cut off, but I finally decided to start going. I joined a yoga class and started belly dancing. It's been fun and I hadn't realized how much I missed and needed some woman energy. Friends are so good to have.

I realized during this time that I am seeking the truth about whom I am and want to own my feelings. I have two boxes in my closet. One has my letters and treasures from Bert and the other is filled with letters from you. When I open the "Harriet and Don" box (just writing that sentence has moved me again) I realize what a treasure our letters have been. Our lives have played out between the lines, I see the story of how a young girl was reaching out to help and was helped in return, by a mother who had just lost her son. I have come to know your whole family and now understand how you have lived through his death.

In the first letters we exchanged we hardly knew each other, just through Bert. However, that is certainly not the case now. I only knew him for two years on this earth, but I knew him immediately when we first met, it was as if we had known each all along. That's how it was

Harriet Bocca

with us, and he knew me before I knew myself. That's what I loved about him, he really believed in and was so loyal to the people he loved. I know it's a rare trait and I have yet to meet another like him. The amazing thing is that out of my two year friendship with him came you, and our incredible bond which has gone on now for over seventeen years. I don't feel like my time with him ended when he died. He has continued through you. I know he will be the first one there when my time is up. Don't you think the missing him part is what gets harder over time? The other mixed feelings I've had of guilt, anger and confusion have subsided, but I still just miss hanging out with him so much. I ALWAYS had fun with Bert Bocca!

I know it's hard for us to talk outside of on paper, but I want you to know that my relationship with you both is priceless to me. You have played a role of friend, but you are also like a mother and father to me. When I read the letters from you, they are filled with so much love, guidance, and acceptance. That's exactly what Bert gave me and I see where he got it from. I have shared my personal being and the deep core of who I am. I thank you for allowing me to. I have always tried to honor what Bert gave me by really trying to live a real life and make it count!

You have helped me be a mother, which can be horrifying at times. Now that Nicolet is a teenager, I recognize her wild spirit, just as I was at her age. I am grateful that she gets good grades, and is super pretty, yet funny and fun to be around. I also remember what it was like as a teenager. I want to protect her and I want her to fly all at the same time. She has her first boyfriend, I make them hang out with me and play Yahtzee, always wanting to supervise them at all times. I know that's not realistic, but I want to be there for her in all ways as she is growing up so fast. I shall try my best; yet at the end of the day, I will have to let her go.

I hope this letter hasn't worn you out, I really needed to say all that. We need to visit...and I hope that it will happen soon.

Love, Holly

Harriet Bocca

March 2008

Wow, Holly you are amazing, so pure. Words cannot possible capture your nature and the complexity of life and our relationship as we evolved together. Our journey has been one only you and I could have taken and one which is not over.

I understand how the combination of being without little Sammy and having cabin fever can wear you down. I'm glad you have gotten involved in outside physical activities with other women, as we women are quite wonderful and the best of friends. I've come to the conclusion that friends come in different categories, each with a special talent of support. One for a reality check, another can be a soft shoulder to cry on, and another who is the one that wants to help fix! Put them all together and you have a great support system. I'm glad you have your sisters too, for they can be the best friends in the world.

You need to know how very proud you make me feel, your memories of my son are inspiring. He wasn't perfect, he made lots of mistakes, but I know he was kind and I know he loved you. He recognized your sweetness and kindness as well. Perhaps you were meant to be connected forever. Perhaps your connections would not have been so strong if he hadn't died so young. The need to keep his memory alive is so obvious as others might forget.

Nicolet sounds so typical for a teenage girl, what a great age! I guess you could try to lock her in her room, but that won't stop her from being the wonderful young curious woman you raised. Anyway, it sounds like she could figure out how to break out!

One last thing, before I go. A while back, you mentioned that you loved the movie Juno. While I haven't seen it yet, I understand it's about a young girl who became pregnant before she was married and had to face hard decisions. I have never told you but I too was pregnant before marriage, so I could certainly relate. Don and I were seventeen and planned on getting married, but hadn't set a date. Remember, we were young, dumb and in lust. Sound familiar? We broke up for a short while; we were both far too immature and not ready. Since this was in the early sixties, in society's eyes I was considered a bad girl. I was brought up in a strict Catholic home, where we were taught that, "good girls don't have sex before marriage." I became desperate as the months passed, not knowing what to do, afraid and ashamed to tell my parents. Yet I had to eventually as I obviously began to show. I never considered an abortion; it was not an option for me. I finally told my parents and they were wonderful. My Dad was sitting in the living room, which is where so much life took place, he asked me to sit on his lap, much like I had when I was just a little girl. He gave me a big hug and told me he would always love me, and that things "would work out." Things did work out, and Don and I were married shortly after that. Our wedding was nothing fancy mind you, just a small church wedding and a family reception at my parents' house. My mom made meatloaf and salads and Don's mom furnished the store bought cake. I am often amazed at the money spent on lavish weddings and then a few years later the couple is divorced. I think couples should have the big celebration of their wedding around the 10 year anniversary; it would

Harriet Bocca

give the couple something to work for and at least a reason to stay together. After all, who would want to miss a great party and after ten years you really can use new towels or a toaster. By the way, both Don and I recognize that the human body is made to have sex at an early age, as our purpose is to procreate and continue the human race. The act of sex seems so natural. Deep, committed love is an ongoing activity which takes serious work as it evolves. In a few years, we will celebrate our 50th anniversary, so it says something about our commitment to each other. I hope Don and I have helped each other become better people along the way, not just stuck together but growing together.

Through the years I have wondered how life would have been if I hadn't gotten pregnant. Would we have ever married? Now I know I have never met another man I would have wanted to spend my life with and travel on this journey.

Love, Harriet

October 2008

Hello dear Holly,

It's such a beautiful time of the year, as the cold nights and shorter days seem to be putting things to bed for the winter. I always think of you and how the cold weather in Idaho turns the leaves the color of fire. I can picture you on your front porch or going for a walk enjoying nature and trying to soak up the last moments of warm sunshine. I'm sure your outside activities become busy with gathering wood, stocking up and getting ready for the winter snow. It's time to start thinking about the upcoming holidays and playing in the snow.

Our summer was far too busy, but filled with lots of memory-making fun activities. I don't think most understand how organized we have to be in order to pack and be on the road continually. That's why we've started to back off and try to take it a little easier. Since the winter months are down time for us, we have learned to slip into a simple lifestyle. Of course, I still have a commitment as a Court Appointed Special Advocate (CASA), but I'm pretty much able to schedule my time. By the way, it has been an extremely rewarding activity. I have learned a lot about how a child who has been abused becomes the abuser as an adult, or accepts abuse in absence of structured security, relating the abuse to love. It becomes a cycle without end. The good news is that there are those who make it and do something positive with their lives. This last year I've been working with a little girl who has been placed with potential adoptive parents. They have been through an emotional roller coaster with her, yet did not give up. They have worked hard on specific issues and will soon succeed in legally becoming her parents, which has been their dream. I have witnessed such growth in her since her placement with this family. With their loving support and arms wrapped around her, she will achieve anything she sets her mind too and then some.

Since work slows down this time of the year, we've started some projects around the house. It seems like we are never finished

Harriet Bocca

with all that needs to be done, I sometimes wonder if we avoid finishing so we'll always have something, a reason to keep going. This week Don has been cleaning the garage, believe me it needed it! When we moved up here, our furniture and boxes were stored in our storage container while we lived in our little travel trailer. Then as the house was being built, we stored our belongings in the basement/garage. Now after eight years Don is bringing up the boxes, which were in the far corners of the garage. You know what that means; I get to go through those memories! We have so many photos of another life, and our story unfolds through the years in the long ago photos. I realize that we are the only ones who know the circumstances behind the lens. I've spent hours writing on the backs of photos, trying to document names and dates, it's my way of validating that we had a good life filled with happiness and sorrow. Many of the photos of Brandon and Bert brought back the moment and lifted my heart. Soon we hope to put them on the computer and organize the files. Going through these treasured memories reminded me of the one thing that I have always know, that our kids all had great childhoods. Perhaps that knowledge has helped me cope with the tragedy of losing Brandon and Bert. I keep thinking that nobody wants all this stuff, (baby booties, old hats, even a great collection of sport shirt and of course school records and documents,) I can't bear to let go of them. I picture Laurence and Anne going through these cherished memories and reliving life with their brothers, I hope it's not too hard on them, as reality of what they have lost could overwhelm them. Perhaps they will feel comforted by the good memories, and share with their children part of their past which made them who they are.

I hope you and Tony haven't been affected by the "economic depression," it's been hard on a lot of people and I hope things turn around soon. I feel so bad for young families with children, just going grocery shopping can be overwhelming. Perhaps more people should take a lesson from you and at least plant a small vegetable garden. Our son Laurence, who has worked for the same company for over twenty years, was let go last month. He was one of the last to go before the company closed their doors for good. With two teenagers to support by himself and no health insurance, it's tough. We're grateful that he has a great attitude and was smart enough to have some savings set aside. He and the girls have cut where they can, and we can only hope this too will end. I know that your Nicolet is now a teenager, so you know what kind of demand that can be on the budget. Perhaps this will be an opportunity for my grandchildren to learn about doing with less. Guess we all can learn something.

All my love, Harriet

(Letter not mailed but continued later)

November 2008

Hi Holly, I'm back,

I started this letter in October and am finally getting back to it. As you know, life gets in the way and is filled with distractions, some fun some not so fun. We are now in Palm Desert, enjoying warm balmy days. While I love Summer Lake most of the year, it was fortunate that we were able to find a small house down here in the lower desert of

Harriet Bocca

California for the winter. As we grow older, the cold winters in the high mountains were getting more difficult on our bodies. We do better when it's a little warmer. It's a lifestyle change with sidewalks, street lights, cars and all kinds of noises, but fun to enjoy the newness and variety of people.

Looks like we'll be having Thanksgiving Dinner out this year, that's a first! Laurence and the girls will join us at a local restaurant. Guess I'll have to roast a turkey later, we really love the leftovers. We hope to travel to Sacramento sometime during the Christmas holiday. Since Laurence is out of work, we will all be together at our daughter's home for the first time in years. See, there is good from being out of work; it's an opportunity to be together for the holidays! It's not exactly a paid vacation, but it is time off.

We hope you have a wonderful holiday season, please let us know if you will be able to come down to the desert, it would be great to see you.

Love, Harriet

December 2008

Dear Harriet,

Got your letter the other day, stashed it away until I could be alone to read it. A ritual when I get anything from you.

I'm sorry I have not written you since my stressful letter last winter. I know I worried you. Things are much improved since then. Tony and I have seemed to have found each other again. I've learned that marriage is hard work, but a good marriage is the biggest reward. We both have made the commitment to live happier, healthier lives together. I am reminded that life can be great.

As you know, we have been trying to live a cleaner life, one without chemicals, pesticides, and processed foods. I've recently gone into an online business which sells only green products. I have passion about this product, and am excited at the prospect of being in business for myself.

Nicolet is great, beautiful, smart and fun to be around. She will soon turn seventeen and has already had her heart broken, but is moving on. I believe she realizes that this too shall pass, but it's a hard lesson to learn. I am in awe, watching her go through the changes from childhood to her own person, obviously aware how quickly life can change by making bad choices. As a parent, I do a lot of praying.

Sammy, who turned six on Bert's Birthday, is the perfect boy. He gives me so much mom love and is always willing to give me big hugs and kisses. It is amazing how different my two children are. Nicolet was independent at an early age, and Sammy still wants mommy to comfort him, be with him, and just be there. He loves Star Wars and Legos, not kindergarten so much. Like most boys, he would rather be running free or building something, anything. I am told he is a natural leader; boys and girls are drawn to him. I know he will find his place in this world and whatever it may be, I will always be proud of both of my children.

I continue to explore my own journey with an open heart, always welcoming truth and love in my life. Recently I spent twenty four hours with two of my best girlfriends from high school. It had been almost fifteen years since we had all been together, it was so very good to see them and reconnect. After Bert died, I made a conscious decision to distance myself from those old memories and focus on my goals in life. I guess you could call it growing up. Our get-together, slumber party was a visit of another time, a time when we felt invincible and free. Bert's death changed all that, as we recognize how fragile life can be. Each one of us has gone on with our lives, yet none of us will ever forget. Every time I write I tell myself I will not bring up Bert, but I have yet to accomplish that. I still feel very connected to him and am so grateful for his gift to me of you.

Now that my kids are growing up, I am faced with figuring out what I want to do when I grow up! I do some volunteering at an after school program. While this is rewarding, I find what my heart desires to do with my time does not usually make any money. Tony works so hard, and I would love to help with our finances. Perhaps my new internet marketing of green products will be just what the doctor ordered. I believe in the product, as it will be something which will help people and bring a little extra income for the family. Working from home will allow me to continue to be the best mommy I can be and as you have done, have dinner ready when my hard-working husband comes home.

 Time to go; the kids will be home from school soon.

I love you, Holly

A Visit with Holly

The October air was cool as we got out of the truck and stood in the driveway of Holly's house. Fall comes early in the high country of Idaho; causing the leaves to turn golden orange with blankets of red. It was beautiful. I shivered slightly, not out of cold but anticipation. There she stood, looking much as she did when we first met. Her hair long and falling softly to her shoulders, no noticeable make up, just a fresh and clean look. As I approached the porch she came forward. I detected a few wrinkles around her eyes, something she had not had those long years ago when my son first introduced us. The forming of tears was noticeable as our emotional journey seemed to have come full circle.

The moment so long in coming was surreal. As we hugged, a dog, barking in the distance, broke the silence. It was as if we had not been apart. Her house was modest, with all the signs of a busy life filled with work and play. Some of Sammy's toys were on the front porch and a neatly stacked woodpile nearby, in wait of winter quickly approaching. Deer droppings were all over the grass as we entered her garden. It had a six-foot high fence surrounding the perimeter and an old metal gate to enter. The fence was somewhat effective in keeping the deer out of her garden, but I don't know how she kept the bears out! Dying pumpkin vines, which had once been deep green were now drawing back into the warm soil, in a last ditch effort to continue.

Holly's Home and Garden

Words Spoken Only On Paper

A trellis of vines ran the distance of her backyard garden, remnants of the dark colored huckleberry and raspberry bushes, which she harvested earlier in the season. While Holly had sent many photos of her garden through the years, as well as homemade jam and jellies made from those very vines, actually being there was more than I had envisioned.

Since she often wrote about her love of her garden, I was anxious to walk through to experience firsthand, her special place. It was almost intimate, as we strolled up and down the rows, she pointing out the variety of vegetables she had planted, and I amazed at the work she had put into it. Her enthusiasm and pride were obvious, so was the peace she seemed to express in the very way she talked about each plant. Because it was late in the season, little was left of her harvest, only a few cherry tomatoes and pumpkins waiting to be picked. Carefully placed ceramic and wooden fantasy fairies were tucked into small corners and recesses along the path, as though they were keepers of her garden. Miniature fairytale scenes peeking out from under hidden places left my imagination wondering just what these magical creatures might be doing.

My visit with Holly was twofold, and I definitely had a mission. Of course, I was excited to see her and her family. I had met her husband a number of times and he was always welcoming. He has a calmness about him, perhaps it's from years of living, and working in such a peaceful quiet place As we entered the living room, the aroma of spaghetti sauce he had started earlier in the day wafted through the air. It was a familiar smell, one of a home. There was a wood burning stove, in the living room, which Holly said they keep burning all winter long. The house was neat and cozy with plenty of light coming in from the windows, and some of Holly's arts and crafts decorated the walls. As I looked out the kitchen window, I could see the forest, with plenty of pine trees and evergreens surrounding a large clearing, which lead to the dog's pen. In a huge tree, there was a wood fort, made for Sammy, but I bet enjoyed by the whole family. It gave me comfort to know they had dogs. Not only are dogs man's best friend, they are also great protectors. Since Holly lives in the forest and so do wild animals, dogs are a perfect deterrent for those wild animals coming too close.

Each room in her house was filled with life, from Sammy's collection of Legos, which he has made into incredible structures (some even move), to Nicolet's, pastel colored walls, with posters depicted her favorite musical groups. This room will soon change, as Nicolet will be off to college, and each time she returns home she will bring bits and pieces of her new grown-up life. I know that this will be a difficult time for Holly. She will struggle with the fact that her first child, her only daughter is growing up. In her heart she will want this child of hers to fly, but that same heart will never want to see her go too far.

The second part of my mission and something I had to do in person was to deliver this manuscript to Holly. While there was some changing and editing of her original letters, the essence of her private thoughts and trusted words to me were kept intact. Our growth together and our special bond will never end. I respect her, just as I know my son did. There is not one person alive who does not have a story to tell.

Together Holly and I have told a part of ours, and hope you the reader will learn as we have that life can go on for those left behind, and it can be a happy, wonderful full life. We're not done yet, just continue reading.

January 2010

Dear Harriet,

I'm in bed, its 19 degrees out, considerably warmer than the past two weeks. It's 12:20am and officially my daughters 18th birthday! She is in Seattle, Washington on the first leg of a birthday trip that will take her to California before she comes home. She will be graduating in June and then moving to Southern California to go to college. My heart is breaking and so full of joy all at once! I suppose that's the term "bitter sweet." She is amazing and smart and has made really good decisions. I know she honors herself. Does that mean I did a good job? I was 18 when she was born and I couldn't imagine her expecting a child and being a mother right now. Thinking of that time in my life inevitably leads to thoughts of Bert and the girl I was.

I have known always that this time, a birth and a death, both beloved was the most defining moment of my life. In one single moment in time, everything changed. My whole perception of myself, the people who mattered, God, death, life, mortality and in the end, hope, love, and faith changed forever, right then and there. My true journey began and I began to find myself on purpose!

It has been an amazing adventure so far and I'm still looking. I think of the choices I have made and wonder how different things would be if he had lived. I have had your manuscript beside me and I have had it for way too long. I'm sorry for that. I can't seem to deal with it. Its right on page two that I can't get past. Six words..."the loud ringing of the phone." I know what follows on the next pages and I don't want to go there. I'm thinking of my own phone call. I was with a bunch of girlfriends at one of their parents 'houses and the phone rang. One of the girls answered (I really wasn't paying attention), and then everyone was kind of staring at me. As she came towards me, she was crying. It seemed like slow motion, but there was no stopping it from happening. That was the moment it happened, the girl I was, was gone! I now had inside information that we don't have a golden ticket in life. I found out that moment that life is fragile and that maybe life doesn't go on and on until you're old and grey. I had to look at myself. I had to eventually forgive myself too for being so self-centered and for taking the big, important things for granted. Soon after that, I started changing my life. I knew it was time to grow up

    The birth of my beautiful daughter was like a crash course and it truly helped me be a better person. She has taught me so many lessons that now help sustain me. It taught me about love and true friendship, about kindness and compassion. It gave me the bravery to have dreams and to allow myself to look for myself. It taught me how precious every moment is, to be present. It opened a door that brought me to know God.

I just felt a pang of guilt for getting so many amazing gifts from Bert, and he not getting to be here. However, I think he loves us all that much, and his life was his gift. That of course brings me to thoughts of you. The safe, beautiful place you have given me over almost twenty years now has been priceless to me. It has allowed me to not dwell in "THAT" place for too long and allowed me to care for others in my life.

So, I am going to stop being fearful and follow through with your manuscript. I know it will change me a little too, as all-important things do. I will pray and give thanks for my beautiful daughter as she starts her own journey. May she know the love I have.

Love, me

Dear Reader

Our evolution continues. I recently received a beautiful letter from Nicolet, thanking us for sending a high school graduation gift. She looks so much like her mother in the photograph she sent. When I first met Holly those many years ago, she was not quite eighteen, yet one who possessed a maturity of the woman she was soon to become. Her daughter, like her, possesses those same traits. Her long brown hair, which highlights her dark brown eyes and unassuming smiles, gives the unsuspecting stranger a sense of peacefulness. It's the same face of a fragile teenager girl yet possesses an elusive strength, just like her mother. My son must have recognized this strength those many years ago, as he insisted I meet her, he must have known we would need each other someday.

The years have flown by yet they have stood still for me; I know that Holly and I will always be in each other's thoughts. Her beautiful sensitive letters have become fewer and shorter each year, as it should be. Our parallel lives of mutual longing will continue as we grow into the women we were meant to become. Holly and I were destined to stay connected. Bert would have liked that.

The End?

Harriet Bocca

Not quite!

An email from Holly

The last twenty years sort of melt together and the things I've said are unclear to me. It's such a big part of our lives to get on paper and to also have meaning for others. You know, as of late, Bert has been in my heart as Peter Pan and his desire to not grow up and stay fun and adventurous, he lives on for so many as that symbol. The story is complete with his loyal group of Lost Boys, Never Never Land and of course Wendy, who ultimately can't stay there with him and goes on and grows up and has children of her own. But Peter is there to remind us of the gift of staying childlike and the Truth that even though these bodies of ours grow old and tired, it's our Spirit that holds who we are. I am in awe of the never-ending Circle of life and love and Friendship and the journey into the Mystery. I love you!

Holly

Now that you've read my story, perhaps you will be inspired to take the time to write a letter to someone special.

If you close your eyes and listen to your heart, the words will be true.

Love, Harriet

CPSIA information can be obtained at www.ICGtesting.com
Printed in the USA
LVOW071544140112

263708LV00003B/6/P